SECOND EDITION

In Christ's Service

A Concise Biblical Approach

David Wayne Meeker

SECOND EDITION

IN CHRIST'S SERVICE

A Concise Biblical Approach

David Wayne Meeker

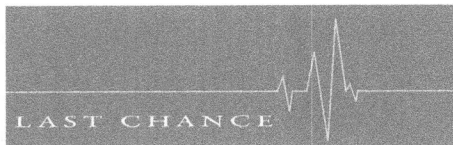

Published by Last Chance Music Ministry

ELEVATION PRESS
OF COLORADO

In Christ's Service: A Concise Biblical Approach
by David Wayne Meeker

Published by Last Chance Music Ministry, Hutto, Texas
2nd Edition, 2025

Editing services provided by Laura Diane Meeker of Last Chance Music Ministry and Don Benjamin of Elevation Press of Colorado.

Cover and interior design and formatting by Donna Marie Benjamin of Elevation Press of Colorado.

Front cover photo: 4th Century mosaic art depicting *Loaves and Fish* (Public Domain)
Back cover photo: Laura Diane Meeker

David & Laura Meeker
lastchancemusic1@aol.com

Ordering information: Quantity sales. Special discounts are available on quantity purchases by book clubs, corporations, associations, and others. For details, contact the publisher at the address above.

ISBN 979-8-9853834-5-4

1. Main category — [Bible] 2. Other categories — [Theology, Doctrine] — [Discipleship]

δοξάζω **(doxazó)** Usage: The verb primarily means to glorify or to give glory. In the New Testament, it is used to describe the act of giving honor and praise to God, acknowledging His majesty, power, and divine nature. It also refers to the glorification of Jesus Christ, particularly in the context of His resurrection and ascension.

Truth Charts®
Copyright © 2014
by David Wayne Meeker
All rights reserved.

Last Chance Music Ministry
lastchancemusic1@aol.com

Presented to:

_____

By:

_____

On:

_____

．～✦～．

This book is dedicated to our daughter, Kristie.

．～✦～．

Contents

Acknowledgments

The first and most important acknowledgment I could ever make is recognizing the eternal, life-changing impact which my Lord and Savior Jesus Christ has made in my life for both time and eternity.

I want to thank my wife, Laura, for all her encouragement while writing this book. I am so honored to be called her husband. She is a lover of Jesus Christ and an example of a follower being *In Christ's Service*. Also, I want to thank both my dad and mom, Doug and Lynn, for their Christian example of Christ's love that they have displayed so clearly in my life. I also want to thank my dad, my wife, and Don Paul Benjamin for editing this book and our daughter, Kristie, and Donna Marie Benjamin for graphic arts. To God be all the praise, glory, and honor!

In Christ's Service Creed

I will first present this important creed without citations so the reader may fully focus on the words. Then I will repeat the creed with applicable Biblical citations so that the reader may come to recognize that this creed is completely based upon the Bible.

We believe that the Bible is the inspired Word of God and is profitable for doctrine, for reproof, for correction, for instruction in righteousness. We believe the Bible is true, perfect, and the sole source of all truth pertaining to the personal attributes and characteristics of God, the condition of man, and His plan of redemption. We believe the Bible should be studied, obeyed, and shared. We believe that God is eternal, God is Love, God is Spirit, God is One, and God cannot lie. We believe God knows all things. We believe God is the Creator and Sustainer of the universe. We believe that God created man in His own image. We believe that God created the Earth, solar system, and everything in it in six literal days and rested on the seventh day. We believe that the name of satan translated as Lucifer, in some older versions of the Bible, is an incorrect translation, and should have been translated as "star of the morning, son of the dawn." We believe that sin originated in Heaven by satan who was cast down to earth. We believe that sin and death entered the world through Adam's disobedience. We believe that through his disobedience, sin and death passed on to all men. We believe there is one God revealed in three persons, the Father, Son, and Holy Spirit. We believe that Jesus Christ is the Son of God and the second person of the Trinity, being the eternal God and equal in substance to the Father and Holy Spirit and took upon Himself the nature of a man with all the essential properties and common infirmities but without sin. We believe He was conceived by the Holy Spirit and born of a virgin, being fully God and fully man with two whole perfect and distinct natures, the Godhead and manhood. We believe Jesus was sent by God the Father as our Sacrifice and Savior from everlasting punishment in hell. We believe that Jesus Christ suffered and died on a cross and was buried and rose again on the third day bodily and appeared to over five hundred witnesses. We believe Jesus ascended to Heaven and sits at the right hand of the Father and will return in the same manner He ascended. We believe that Jesus will judge both the living and the dead. We believe Jesus Christ is the only mediator between God and men. We believe that salvation is a gift from God and a work of the Holy Spirit and comes by grace through faith in Jesus Christ as we repent of our sin and abide in Christ. We believe that baptism symbolizes the death, burial, and resurrection of our Lord Jesus Christ and is important but not necessary for salvation. We believe that a new believer should be baptized as an act of obedience. We believe that the sacrifice of Christ alone was and is sufficient for our sin. We believe we need God to know God. We believe that a change occurs in the heart of a person who comes to Christ, and his or her desires and motives will thus glorify God and not himself or herself. We believe faith is dead without works. We believe that a disciple will always struggle with sin in this life but is justified and sanctified and has no condemnation in Christ. We believe that a disciple will obey God, pray to God, worship God, and praise God. We believe a disciple will abide in Christ, practice righteousness, remain pure, not habitually sin, and overcome the world. We believe that a disciple will share the Gospel, make other disciples, and baptize and teach them the commands of Christ. We believe today is the day of salvation. We believe that disciples will love their neigh-

bors, and will seek fellowship with other disciples in unity. We believe that disciples will deny themselves, carry their cross, and follow Jesus. We believe that disciples will love God with all their heart, mind, soul, and strength; rightly divide the Word of truth; be ready to give an answer for the hope that is in them with gentleness and respect; be fruitful; and evangelize. We believe that we disciples need to fight the good fight, finish the race, keep the faith, submit, surrender, serve, and obey. We believe that God's grace, mercy, peace, truth, and love abide in us disciples. We believe that at the moment of our physical death, we disciples will be in the presence of the Lord—judged and found innocent through the blood of Christ—and we will live a new life in eternity with God in a new Heaven and a new Earth. Amen.

1. We believe that the Bible is the inspired Word of God and is profitable for doctrine, for reproof, for correction, for instruction in righteousness (2 Ti. 3:16).

2. We believe the Bible is true (Ps. 33:24), perfect (Ps. 18:30), and the sole source of all truth pertaining to the personal attributes, characteristics of God, the condition of man (Is. 64:6), and His plan of redemption (Ro. 5:9).

3. We believe the Bible should be studied (2 Ti. 2:15), obeyed (1 Jn. 2:3), and shared (1 Pe. 3:15).

4. We believe that God is eternal (Ps. 45:6), God is Love (1 Jn. 4:8), God is Spirit (Jn. 4:24), God is One, (Is. 46:9; Ga. 3:20), and God cannot lie (Tit. 1:2).

5. We believe God knows all things (Ps. 147:9).

6. We believe God is the Creator and Sustainer of the universe (Is. 40:28; He. 1:3).

7. We believe that God created man in His own image (Ge. 1:27).

8. We believe that God created the earth, solar system, and everything in it (Col. 1:16) in six literal days (Ge. 1:31) and rested on the seventh day (Ge. 2:2).

9. We believe that the name of satan translated as Lucifer in some older versions of the Bible is an incorrect translation, and should have been translated as *"star of the morning, son of the dawn"* (Is. 14:12).

10. We believe that sin originated in Heaven by satan, whose name in Hebrew is actually *"star of the morning, son of the dawn,"* who was cast down to earth by God (Is. 14:12-15).

11. We believe that sin and death entered the world through Adam's disobedience (Ge. 3:1, 6; Ro. 5:19).

12. We believe that through Adam's disobedience, sin and death passed on to all men (Ro. 5:12).

13. We believe there is one God revealed in three persons: Father, Son, and Holy Spirit (Mt. 3:16-17; 1 Pe. 1:2).

14. We believe that Jesus Christ is the Son of God (1 Jn. 4:15) and the second person of the Trinity (1 Jn. 5:7), being the eternal God and equal in substance (Col. 2:9) to the Father and Holy Spirit, and took upon Himself the nature of a man (Ph. 2:8) with all the essential properties and common infirmities but without sin (2 Co. 5:21).

15. We believe He was conceived by the Holy Spirit (Mt. 1:18) and born of a virgin (Lu. 1:27), being fully God and fully man with two whole, perfect, and distinct natures: the Godhead and manhood (Col. 2:9).

16. We believe Jesus was sent by God the Father as our Sacrifice (Jn. 3:16) and Savior (Jn. 3:17; 2 Th. 1:8, 9) from everlasting punishment (Mt. 25:48) in hell (Mt. 25:41; Ro. 6:23).

17. We believe that Jesus Christ suffered (1 Pe. 4:1) and died on a cross and was buried and rose again on the third day bodily and appeared to over five hundred witnesses (1 Co. 15:2-6).

18. We believe Jesus ascended to Heaven and sits at the right hand of the Father (Mk. 16:19) and will return in the same manner He ascended (Ac. 1:10, 11).

19. We believe that Jesus will judge both the living and the dead (Jn. 5:22; Ac. 10:42).

20. We believe Jesus Christ is the only mediator between God and men (1 Ti. 2:5).

21. We believe that salvation is a gift from God (Ep. 2:8, 9; 1 Jn. 5:11, 12) and a work of the Holy Spirit (Jn. 16:8-11) and comes by grace

through faith in Jesus Christ (Ro. 3:24; Col. 1:14) as we repent of our sins (Mk. 1:15; Lu. 13:3) and abide in Christ (2 Jn. 1:9).

22. We believe that baptism symbolizes the death, burial, and resurrection of our Lord Jesus Christ (Col. 2:12) and is important but not necessary for salvation (Mk. 16:16; Lu. 7:50; 23:43).

23. We believe that a new believer should be baptized as an act of obedience (Ac. 2:38).

24. We believe that the sacrifice of Christ alone was and is sufficient for our sin (2 Co. 5:21; Ep. 2:8, 9; 1 Jn. 1:7).

25. We believe we need God to know God (Jn. 6:44; 1 Co. 2:14).

26. We believe that a change occurs in the heart of a person who comes to Christ (Ro. 12:2; 2 Co. 5:17), and his or her desires and motives will thus glorify God and not himself or herself (Jn. 3:30; 2 Co. 1:12).

27. We believe faith is dead without works (Ja. 2:17).

28. We believe that a disciple will always struggle with sin in this life (Ro. 7:15-25) but is justified (Ac. 13:39), sanctified (He. 10:10), and has no condemnation in Christ (Ro. 8:1).

29. We believe that a disciple will obey God (Jn. 10:27; 14:15), pray to God (Ep. 6:18), worship God (Ex. 34:14), and praise God (Ps. 150:1-6).

30. We believe a disciple will abide in Christ (Jn. 15:4-8; Col. 2:6), practice righteousness (1 Jn. 3:7), remain pure (1 Jn. 5:18), not habitually sin (Ro. 6:1; 1 Jn. 3:9), and overcome the world (1 Jn. 4:4; 5:5).

31. We believe that a disciple will share the Gospel (Ep. 3:8), make other disciples, baptize (Mt. 28:19), and teach them the commands of Christ (Mt. 28:20).

32. We believe today is the day of salvation (2 Co. 6:2).

33. We believe that disciples will love their neighbors (Mt. 22:39), love other disciples (Jn. 13:34, 35) and will seek fellowship with them in love and unity (He. 10:25).

34. We believe that disciples will deny themselves, carry their cross, and follow Jesus (Mt. 16:24).

35. We believe that a disciple will love God with all his or her heart, mind, soul, and strength (Mk. 12:30), rightly divide the Word of truth (2 Ti. 2:15), and will be ready to give an answer for the hope that is in him or her with gentleness and respect (1 Pe. 3:15), be fruitful (Jn. 15:5-8), and evangelize (Mt. 28:18-20).

36. We believe that we disciples need to fight the good fight, finish the race, and keep the faith (2 Ti. 4:7), submit (Ja. 4:7), surrender (1 Pe. 5:7), serve (Col. 3:24), and obey (Lu. 11:28).

37. We believe that God's grace, mercy, peace, truth, and love abide in us disciples (2 Jn. 1:2, 3).

38. We believe that at the moment of our physical death, we disciples will be in the presence of the Lord (2 Co. 5:8), judged (He. 9:27), and found innocent through the blood of Christ (Jn. 10:28; Re. 1:5); and we will live a new life in eternity (Jn. 3:16; Ro. 6:23) with God (Re. 22:3, 4) in a new Heaven and a new Earth (Is. 65:17; 1 Co. 2:9; 2 Pe. 3:13; Re. 21:1-4). Amen.

Introduction

This book is for men and women, both young and old, everywhere, who have a desire to draw closer to God and learn what the Bible has to say about being *In Christ's Service*. The Bible is very clear about what it means to be *In Christ's Service* and why. How can we apply this significant Biblical truth to our daily lives? I address these extremely important questions in a simple and concise Biblical format in my book, *In Christ's Service*.

As for your own questions, I'm sure you're probably asking at this point who am I? Let me begin to answer this question by saying who I am not. I am not a theologian, pastor, or a Bible teacher; but I have a desire to know and study God's Word and share it with others. I'm not an evangelist, although I have a desire to share the Gospel of Jesus Christ with a lost and dying world.

Now, you might be asking, "If you're not a theologian, pastor, teacher, or an evangelist, then why are you writing a book about the Christian faith?" The answer is this: I am a disciple of Jesus Christ, and because I am a disciple of Jesus Christ in His service, indwelt by the Holy Spirit, it makes sense that I would feel the same way about Christian faith as God does.

Two of the necessary requirements, which are among several, for being *In Christ's Service* are 1) the acceptance and assistance of spreading the Gospel, and 2) learning and obeying Christ's teachings. As Christians we must understand that we need God to know God; and knowing Him means that any desire that we may have to please and serve God with our lives actually comes from God, and the lack of it does not (1 Co. 2:14).

Since this statement is true, why do so many Christians lack a desire to please and serve God with their lives? I realize there can only be two possible reasons for this situation: Either it's the result of 1) false conversion as outlined by Christ in the Parable of the Sower in Luke 8:11-15, or 2) the result of a true conversion struggling with the sinful nature as described by the Apostle Paul in Romans 7:15-25.

It is this simple premise that compelled me to write this book. I do not seek to judge the Body of Christ unrighteously or hypocritically. Rather, I seek to use the Word of God as a tool to better serve the Body of Christ by helping those who seek an authentic relationship with God through Jesus Christ to better understand God's Truth. Throughout this book, I'll be using the Bible as my primary-source document in obtaining Biblically correct answers on this topic.

Every follower of Jesus Christ needs to understand what it means to be *In Christ's Service.* Christ said in Mark 8:34, "Whoever desires to come after Me, let him deny himself, and take up his cross, and follow Me" (NKJV); and in Mark 12:30 we read that He said, "you shall love the Lord your God with all your heart, with all your soul, with all your mind, and with all your strength" (NKJV).

What does it mean to be a disciple *In Christ's Service?* Let's search the Scriptures together and see what God has to say! To adequately answer this question, we will need to look at eight specific categories in Scripture. In the first category we will briefly discuss and establish the reliability and trustworthiness of the Bible, and this will provide a dependable foundation for the seven remaining categories. The evidence will show, beyond a shadow of a doubt, that the reliability and trustworthiness of the Bible is the result of Divine origin rather than human origin and can be fully trusted.

The categories that will be discussed are as follows:

1. The Bible   5. Fellowship
2. Obedience   6. Evangelism
3. Prayer   7. Discipleship
4. Worship & Praise   8. Baptism

While you're traveling down this narrow path of improved Biblical understanding, don't forget that a follower of Jesus Christ is justified (Ac. 13:39), sanctified (He. 10:10), and has no condemnation in Christ (Ro. 8:1)! Hallelujah! At the same time, we need to understand what God has to say about being *In Christ's Service* so that we can better serve and please Him with our lives. We must know what God requires and expects from us, not to satisfy some requirement for a good-works-based salvation, but out of love and gratitude for His love, grace, mercy, and gift of salvation. He has done everything for us beyond what we could ever conceive or imagine (1 Co. 2:9; Ep. 3:20).

My only motive for writing this book comes from the love I have for God, the Body of Christ, and the lost. Please check what I say with Scripture and only hold fast to that which is true. If what I say does not hold true to the Word of God, discard it; but if it does hold true to God's Word, apply it and always remember that the Word of God is the final court of arbitration.

I pray and hope that the information in this book will help bring you to a closer and more intimate relationship with God through our Lord and Savior Jesus Christ, as it has me. God bless you as you discover the Truth found in God's Word. To God be all the glory!

In Christ's Service,
David Wayne Meeker

1. The Bible

Definition:

The Protestant Bible is a collection of sixty-six individual historical documents, thirty-nine of which are called the *Old Testament* and twenty-seven are called the *New Testament*. *"The Bible was written by kings, military leaders, peasants, philosophers, fishermen, tax collectors, poets, musicians, statesmen, scholars, and shepherds over a 1,500-year period on three different continents, Asia, Africa, and Europe, by forty plus authors,"*[1] most who did not even know each other and lived at different times throughout history. It was written in three different languages, Hebrew, Aramaic, and Greek, on thousands of different subjects. Furthermore, it was written without any contradictions and with one central theme claiming Divine inspiration by the Holy Spirit and proving it through statistical and mathematical probability, The Law of Non-Contradiction, eyewitness testimony, logical consistency, predictive and Messianic prophecy, as well as historical, archeological, and scientific evidence. The Bible is unique and unmatched by any other religious book of any other religion in the world, by way of evidential support for its claim of Divine origin and inspiration. There is no logical or reasonable way to explain the Bible's trustworthiness and reliability in its accuracy other than Divine origin and inspiration by the Creator and Sustainer of the universe.

Premise:

The Bible is infinitely important because it is the primary way the Creator communicates His truth to His creation. It reveals the eternally important fact that we need to receive Jesus Christ as Savior and Lord. Without the Bible we would have no personal information about God and His plan of redemption. The actions of an all-loving God Who claims to love a world condemned by sin and without hope are completely consistent with the revealed character of Him as portrayed in Scripture. Also, the very existence of the Bible itself is consistent with the character and nature of a holy, righteous and loving God. The facts are in, and the reality is clear: God sent you and me a message of love. He wants us to submit, serve, and obey Him out of a real, authentic love which is only possible through our submission to the Holy

Spirit. God has given us all the necessary tools to achieve the goal. He gave us the ability to logically reason, He gave us a free will so that we can make honest and sincere choices, and He gave us His Word and the Holy Spirit to help guide us in making right choices as we receive and share His plan of redemption.

Conclusion:

The Bible reveals to us God's love in the most loving act that we could ever experience in this life, namely, by sending His Son as the Sacrifice for the sin of the world. The Bible explains the cause and the effect of our sin and our need for a Savior. When I came to Christ, God gave me the desire to please Him with my life in the things I say, do, and think. I don't always succeed all the time, but through God's love, grace, and mercy I will always have conviction, forgiveness, guidance, and the desire to continue through the work of the Holy Spirit. Because the Bible has proven its reliability and trustworthiness, we know that we can depend on His Word completely about God and His plan of redemption. The Bible is important for us disciples *In Christ's Service* as we learn to understand how to please God with our lives, as we study it and apply it — and an essential part of that is sharing!

Proof Texts:

The Bible is inspired by God.

2 Timothy 3:16, 17

16 All Scripture is inspired by God, and is profitable for teaching, for rebuking, for correcting, for training in righteousness,

17 so that the man of God may be complete, equipped for every good work (HCSB).

The Bible is perfect.

Psalm 18:30

As for God, his way is perfect: The word of Jehovah is tried; He is a shield unto all them that take refuge in him (ASV).

The Bible produces joy.

John 15:11

These things I have spoken to you, that my joy may be in you, and that your joy may be full (ESV).

The Bible gives us comfort.

Psalm 119: 50, 52

50 This is my comfort in my affliction, that your promise gives me life.

52 When I think of your rules from of old, I take comfort, O LORD (ESV).

The Bible gives us hope.

Psalm 119:43

And take not the word of truth utterly out of my mouth, for my hope is in your rules (ESV).

Psalm 119:49

Remember your word to your servant, in which you have made me hope (ESV).

The Bible produces peace.

Psalm 85:8

Let me hear what God the LORD will speak, for he will speak peace to his people, to his saints; but let them not turn back to folly (ESV).

The Bible is right and trustworthy.

Psalm 33:4

For the word of the Lord is right and all His work is trustworthy (HCSB).

The Bible will last forever.

Psalm 119:89

Lord, Your word is forever; it is firmly fixed in heaven (HCSB).

Luke 21:33

Heaven and earth shall pass away: but my words shall not pass away (ASV).

The Bible gives us wisdom.

Psalm 119:99, 100

99 I have more understanding than all my teachers; For thy testimonies are my meditation.

100 I understand more than the aged, Because I have kept thy precepts (ASV).

The Bible can be trusted.

Psalm 119:138

The decrees You issue are righteous and altogether trustworthy (HCSB).

The Bible reveals the truth.

Proverbs 30:5

Every word of God proves true; he is a shield to those who take refuge in him (ESV).

Acts 18:28

For he vigorously refuted the Jews in public, demonstrating through the Scriptures that Jesus is the Messiah (HCSB).

The Bible is holy.

Romans 1:2

which he promised afore through his prophets in the holy scriptures, (ASV).

The Holy Spirit helps us to understand the Bible.

1 Corinthians 2:12-16

12 But we received, not the spirit of the world, but the spirit which is from God; that we might know the things that were freely given to us of God.

13 Which things also we speak, not in words which man's wisdom teacheth, but which the Spirit teacheth; combining spiritual things with spiritual words.

14 Now the natural man receiveth not the things of the Spirit of God: for they are foolishness unto him; and he cannot know them, because they are spiritually judged.

15 But he that is spiritual judgeth all things, and he himself is judged of no man.

16 For who hath known the mind of the Lord, that he should instruct him? But we have the mind of Christ (ASV).

The Bible is to be studied.

2 Timothy 2:15

Give diligence to present thyself approved unto God, a workman that needeth not to be ashamed, handling aright the word of truth (ASV).

The Bible thoroughly equips us.

2 Timothy 3:16, 17

16 All Scripture is breathed out by God and profitable for teaching, for reproof, for correction, and for training in righteousness,

17 that the man of God may be competent, equipped for every good work (ESV).

The Bible is a spiritual weapon.

Ephesians 6:17

And take the helmet of salvation, and the sword of the Spirit, which is the word of God: (ASV).

The Bible is alive and judges our lives.

Hebrews 4:12

For the word of God is living, and active, and sharper than any two-edged sword, and piercing even to the dividing of soul and spirit, of both joints and marrow, and quick to discern the thoughts and intents of the heart (ASV).

The Bible helps us to grow spiritually.

1 Peter 2:2

Like newborn babies, thirst for the pure milk of the word so that by it you may grow in your salvation (ISV).

The Bible gives us guidance.

Psalm 119:105

Thy word is a lamp unto my feet, And light unto my path (ASV).

Psalm 73:23, 24

23 Nevertheless, I am continually with you; you hold my right hand.

24 You guide me with your counsel, and afterward you will receive me to glory (ESV).

Proverbs 6 :23

For the commandment is a lamp and the teaching a light, and the reproofs of discipline are the way of life, (ESV)

The Bible reveals God's will to us.

John 6:38-40

38 For I am come down from heaven, not to do mine own will, but the will of him that sent me.

39 And this is the will of him that sent me, that of all that which he hath given me I should lose nothing, but should raise it up at the last day.

40 For this is the will of my Father, that every one that beholdeth the Son, and believeth on him, should have eternal life; and I will raise him up at the last day (ASV).

1 Peter 2:15

For it is God's will that you, by doing good, silence the ignorance of foolish people (HCSB).

Romans 12:1, 2

1 I beseech you therefore, brethren, by the mercies of God, to present your bodies a living sacrifice, holy, acceptable to God, which is your spiritual service.

2 And be not fashioned according to this world: but be ye transformed by the renewing of your mind, that ye may prove what is the good and acceptable and perfect will of God (ASV).

We can live by the Bible.

Matthew 4:4

But he answered and said, It is written, Man shall not live by bread alone, but by every word that proceedeth out of the mouth of God (ASV).

The Bible says there is no condemnation in Christ.

Romans 8:1

There is therefore now no condemnation to them that are in Christ Jesus (ASV).

The Bible tells us that we are justified through Christ.

Romans 3:24-26

24 being justified freely by his grace through the redemption that is in Christ Jesus:

25 whom God set forth to be a propitiation, through faith, in his blood, to show his righteousness because of the passing over of the sins done aforetime, in the forbearance of God;

26 for the showing, I say, of his righteousness at this present season: that he might himself be just, and the justifier of him that hath faith in Jesus (ASV).

Galatians 2:16

yet knowing that a man is not justified by the works of the law but through faith in Jesus Christ, even we believed on Christ Jesus, that we might be justified by faith in Christ, and not by the works of the law: because by the works of the law shall no flesh be justified (ASV).

The Bible tells us that we are sanctified through Christ.

Hebrews 10:10

By his will we have been sanctified once for all through the sacrifice of the body of Jesus Christ (ISV).

Jesus is called God in the Bible.

John 1:1

In the beginning was the Word, and the Word was with God, and the Word was God (KJV).

John 1:14

And the Word became flesh and dwelt among us, and we have seen his glory, glory as of the only Son from the Father, full of grace and truth (ESV).

John 20:28

And Thomas answered and said unto him, My Lord and my God (KJV).

Romans 9:5

To them belong the patriarchs, and from their race, according to the flesh, is the Christ who is God over all, blessed forever. Amen (ESV).

Titus 2:13

waiting for our blessed hope, the appearing of the glory of our great God and Savior Jesus Christ, (ESV).

Hebrews 1:8

But of the Son he says, "Your throne, O God, is forever and ever, the scepter of uprightness is the scepter of your kingdom" (ESV).

Colossians 2:9

For in him the whole fullness of deity dwells bodily, (ESV).

Jesus claimed to be God.

John 10:27-33

27 "My sheep hear my voice. I know them, and they follow me.

28 I give them eternal life, and they will never perish, and no one will snatch them out of my hand.

29 What my Father has given me is greater than all else, and no one can snatch it from the Father's hand.

30 I and the Father are one."

31 Again the Jews picked up stones to stone him to death.

32 Jesus replied to them, "I have shown you many good works from my Father. For which of them are you going to stone me?"

33 The Jews answered him, "We are not going to stone you for a good work but for blasphemy, because you, a mere man, are making yourself God!" (ISV).

The Bible tells us why Jesus Christ died.

John 3:16-18

16 "For God so loved the world, that he gave his only Son, that whoever believes in him should not perish but have eternal life.

17 For God did not send his Son into the world to condemn the world, but in order that the world might be saved through him.

18 Whoever believes in him is not condemned, but whoever does not believe is condemned already, because he has not believed in the name of the only Son of God" (ESV).

1 Corinthians 15:3

For I delivered unto you first of all that which I also received, how that Christ died for our sins according to the scriptures; (KJV).

1 Peter 3:18

For Christ also hath once suffered for sins, the just for the unjust, that he might bring us to God, being put to death in the flesh, but quickened by the Spirit: (KJV).

Hebrews 9:15

Therefore he is the mediator of a new covenant, so that those who are called may receive the promised eternal inheritance, since a death has occurred that redeems them from the transgressions committed under the first covenant (ESV).

The Bible tells us how to receive faith.

Romans 10:17

So then faith cometh by hearing, and hearing by the word of God (KJV).

The Bible tells us to walk by faith.

2 Corinthians 5:7

for we walk by faith, not by sight (ESV).

The Bible tells us that we are saved by grace through faith.

Ephesians 2:8, 9

8 For by grace you have been saved through faith. And this is not your own doing; it is the gift of God,

9 not a result of works, so that no one may boast (ESV).

The Bible has the power to convict of sin.

Acts 2:37, 38

37 Now when they heard this they were cut to the heart, and said to Peter and the rest of the apostles, "Brothers, what shall we do?"

38 And Peter said to them, "Repent and be baptized every one of you in the name of Jesus Christ for the forgiveness of your sins, and you will receive the gift of the Holy Spirit" (ESV).

The Bible has the power to regenerate.

1 Peter 1:23

since you have been born again, not of perishable seed but of imperishable, through the living and abiding word of God; (ESV).

The Bible gives assurance of eternal life.

1 John 5:11-13

11 And this is the testimony, that God gave us eternal life, and this life is in his Son.

12 Whoever has the Son has life; whoever does not have the Son of God does not have life.

13 I write these things to you who believe in the name of the Son of God that you may know that you have eternal life (ESV).

The Bible says we are free from the law of sin and death in Christ.

Romans 8:2

For the law of the Spirit of life has set you free in Christ Jesus from the law of sin and death (ESV).

The Bible tells us to walk by the Spirit.

Galatians 5:6

But I say, walk by the Spirit, and you will not gratify the desires of the flesh (ESV).

The Bible says the Holy Spirit has the power to renew man.

Titus 3:5

he saved us, not because of works done by us in righteousness, but according to his own mercy, by the washing of regeneration and renewal of the Holy Spirit, (ESV).

The Bible says the Holy Spirit has the power to guide the believer.

John 16:13

When the Spirit of truth comes, he will guide you into all the truth, for he will not speak on his own authority, but whatever he hears he will speak, and he will declare to you the things that are to come (ESV).

The Bible says the Holy Spirit teaches us the Word.

John 14:26

But the Helper, the Holy Spirit, whom the Father will send in my name, he will teach you all things and bring to your remembrance all that I have said to you (ESV).

The Bible tells us to be doers of the Word.

James 1:22

But be doers of the word, and not hearers only, deceiving yourselves (ESV).

The Bible is relevant for our every need today.

Isaiah 40:8

The grass withereth, the flower fadeth: but the word of our God shall stand for ever (KJV).

2 Timothy 3:16, 17

16 All Scripture is breathed out by God and profitable for teaching, for reproof, for correction, and for training in righteousness,

17 that the man of God may be competent, equipped for every good work (ESV).

The Bible tells us why we should memorize God's Word.

Deuteronomy 30:14

But the word is very near you. It is in your mouth and in your heart, so that you can do it (ESV).

Psalm 37:31

The law of his God is in his heart; none of his steps shall slide (KJV).

Psalm 119:11

Thy word have I hid in mine heart, that I might not sin against thee (KJV).

2. Obedience

Definition:

To hear God's Word and act accordingly.

Premise:

Obedience is vitally important! The Bible, as we will see, is very clear on this topic and shows that the love we exhibit toward God the Father is contingent on the level of obedience we have toward Jesus; and the level of love we exhibit toward Jesus is contingent upon the level of obedience we have toward the Holy Spirit. It is through the example of Jesus Christ we learn that believers are called to a life of obedience and that obedience is better than sacrifice.

Conclusion:

By obedience to Christ, we are made partakers through Him in His salvation. The proof that we love Christ is not always determined by the success we have at obeying Him, but rather it is determined by the desire we have to obey Him. I ask God daily to help me please Him with my life in the things I say, do, and think; and I realize that the struggle to please and obey God applies to us all. No one is exempt. The distance between our wickedness and God's righteousness is infinity, and Christ's cross is the only bridge for that gap. Since we need God's help daily to fight the good fight, finish the race, and keep the faith—we must have a desire to seek the Lord daily and submit, surrender, and obey Him out of admiration, affection, and gratefulness. Amen!

Proof Texts:

We are called to obedience.

Deuteronomy 4:1

Now, Israel, listen to the statutes and ordinances I am teaching you to follow, so that you may live, enter, and take possession of the land Yahweh, the God of your fathers, is giving you (HCSB).

Deuteronomy 13:4

Ye shall walk after the LORD your God, and fear him, and keep his commandments, and obey his voice, and ye shall serve him, and cleave unto him (KJV).

1 Peter 1:14-16

[14] As obedient children, do not be shaped by the desires that you once had in your ignorance.

[15] Instead, just as the one who called you is holy, be holy in every aspect of your life.

[16] For it is written, "You must be holy, because I am holy" (ISV).

Obedience is better than sacrifice.

1 Samuel 15:22

Then Samuel said: Does the Lord take pleasure in burnt offerings and sacrifices as much as in obeying the Lord? Look: to obey is better than sacrifice, to pay attention is better than the fat of rams (HCSB).

God gives blessings for obedience.

Exodus 19:5

Now therefore, if ye will obey my voice indeed, and keep my covenant, then ye shall be a peculiar treasure unto me above all people: for all the earth is mine: (KJV).

Deuteronomy 28:1

Now if you faithfully obey the Lord your God and are careful to follow all His commands I am giving you today, the Lord your God will put you far above all the nations of the earth (HCSB).

2 Samuel 24:19

David went up in obedience to God's command, just as the Lord had commanded (HCSB).

Obedience brought blessings beforehand to Abraham.

Genesis 22:18

and in your offspring shall all the nations of the earth be blessed, because you have obeyed my voice (ESV).

Galatians 3:8

Because the Scripture saw ahead of time that God would justify the gentiles by faith, it announced the gospel to Abraham beforehand when it said, "Through you all nations will be blessed" (ISV).

Death came through disobedience, and life came through obedience.

Romans 5:19

For just as through one man's disobedience the many were made sinners, so also through the one man's obedience the many will be made righteous (HCSB).

We can turn from slaves of sin to slaves of God.

Romans 6:16

Don't you know that if you offer yourselves to someone as obedient slaves, you are slaves of that one you obey—either of sin leading to death or of obedience leading to righteousness? (HCSB).

The New Testament says a lot about obedience.

Romans 16:19

The report of your obedience has reached everyone. Therefore, I rejoice over you. But I want you to be wise about what is good, yet innocent about what is evil (HCSB).

Romans 16:26

but now revealed and made known through the prophetic Scriptures, according to the command of the eternal God to advance the obedience of faith among all nations (HCSB).

Philemon 1:21

Since I am confident of your obedience, I am writing to you, knowing that you will do even more than I say (HCSB).

1 Peter 1:2

according to the foreknowledge of God the Father and set apart by the Spirit for obedience and for sprinkling with the blood of Jesus Christ. May grace and peace be multiplied to you (HCSB).

1 Peter 1:22

By obedience to the truth, having purified yourselves for sincere love of the brothers, love one another earnestly from a pure heart, (HCSB).

Romans 2:8

but wrath and indignation to those who are self-seeking and disobey the truth but are obeying unrighteousness; (HCSB).

2 Corinthians 10:5

and every high-minded thing that is raised up against the knowledge of God, taking every thought captive to obey Christ (HCSB).

2 Thessalonians 3:14

And if anyone does not obey our instruction in this letter, take note of that person; don't associate with him, so that he may be ashamed (HCSB).

Hebrews 5:9

After He was perfected, He became the source of eternal salvation for all who obey Him, (HCSB).

1 John 5:2, 3

2 This is how we know that we love God's children when we love God and obey His commands.

3 For this is what love for God is: to keep His commands. Now His commands are not a burden, (HCSB).

John 15:14

You are My friends if you do what I command you (HCSB).

2 John 1:6

And this is love: that we walk according to His commands. This is the command as you have heard it from the beginning: you must walk in love (HCSB).

The proof that Jesus is Lord in our lives is obedience to Him and His Word.

John 14:15

If you love Me, you will keep My commands (HCSB).

Luke 6:46-49

46 "Why do you call me 'Lord, Lord,' and not do what I tell you?

47 Everyone who comes to me and hears my words and does them, I will show you what he is like:

48 he is like a man building a house, who dug deep and laid the foundation on the rock. And when a flood arose, the stream broke against that house and could not shake it, because it had been well built.

49 But the one who hears and does not do them is like a man who built a house on the ground without a foundation. When the stream broke against it, immediately it fell, and the ruin of that house was great" (ESV).

1 John 2:3

This is how we are sure that we have come to know Him: by keeping His commands (HCSB).

John 10:27

My sheep hear my voice. I know them, and they follow me (ISV).

People who obey God's Word will be blessed.

Luke 11:28

But he said, Yea rather, blessed are they that hear the word of God, and keep it (ASV).

Christ was obedient unto death.

Philippians 2:8

And being found in fashion as a man, he humbled himself, becoming obedient even unto death, yea, the death of the cross (ASV).

Peter calls believers in Christ "children of obedience."

1 Peter 1:14

as children of obedience, not fashioning yourselves according to your former lusts in the time of your ignorance: (ASV).

Be a doer—not just a hearer—of the Word.

James 1:22

But be doers of the word, and not hearers only, deceiving yourselves (ESV).

The Holy Spirit is given to those who obey Him.

Acts 5:32

"And we are witnesses to these things, and so is the Holy Spirit, whom God has given to those who obey him" (ESV).

3. Prayer

Definition:

1. A solemn address to the Supreme Being, consisting of adoration, or an expression of our sense of God's glorious perfections, confession of our sins, supplication for mercy and forgiveness, intercession for blessings on others, and thanksgiving, or an expression of gratitude to God for his mercies and benefits.

Premise:

Prayer is critically important to the Christian because it is the primary way that the creation communicates with the Creator. Prayer is an act of humble worship and praise as we seek God with all our heart, mind, soul, and strength. Prayer puts us in the very presence of God and demonstrates our need for God and our hope in Him. Prayer is used for asking God for guidance, direction, and leading. Prayer is used for praising God and includes elements of adoration, confession, and commitment. A lot is accomplished through prayer, and prayer needs to be understood and practiced.

Conclusion:

Pray boldly, and be confident that God knows what is best for you. Go to Him in faith knowing that He hears and answers all your prayers with yes, no, and wait; and in everything give thanks to the Lord, with sincerity, honor, and humbleness. Pray for God's will to be done in your life today, tomorrow, and forever; for He is worthy! Amen!

Proof Texts:

We need to ask God for help.

Psalm 40:13

Be pleased, O LORD, to deliver me: O LORD, make haste to help me (KJV).

God does not hear our prayers if we are habitually sinning.

Micah 3:4

Then shall they cry unto Jehovah, but he will not answer them; yea, he will hide his face from them at that time, according as they have wrought evil in their doings (ASV).

John 9:31

Now we know that God heareth not sinners: but if any man be a worshipper of God, and doeth his will, him he heareth (KJV).

We need to pray with an attitude of humility.

Luke 18:9-14

9 He also told this parable to some who trusted in themselves that they were righteous, and treated others with contempt:

10 "Two men went up into the temple to pray, one a Pharisee and the other a tax collector.

11 The Pharisee, standing by himself, prayed thus: 'God, I thank you that I am not like other men, extortioners, unjust, adulterers, or even like this tax collector.

12 I fast twice a week; I give tithes of all that I get.'

13 But the tax collector, standing far off, would not even lift up his eyes to heaven, but beat his breast, saying, 'God, be merciful to me, a sinner!'

14 I tell you, this man went down to his house justified, rather than the other. For everyone who exalts himself will be humbled, but the one who humbles himself will be exalted" (ESV).

Prayer should not be a show.

Matthew 6:6

But when you pray, go into your room and shut the door and pray to your Father who is in secret. And your Father who sees in secret will reward you (ESV).

Jesus taught His disciples how to pray.

Matthew 6:9-13

9 After this manner therefore pray ye: Our Father which art in heaven, Hallowed be thy name.

10 Thy kingdom come. Thy will be done in earth, as it is in heaven.

11 Give us this day our daily bread.

12 And forgive us our debts, as we forgive our debtors.

13 And lead us not into temptation, but deliver us from evil: For thine is the kingdom, and the power, and the glory, forever. Amen (KJV).

We need to pray in Jesus' Name.

Ephesians 5:20

Giving thanks always for all things unto God and the Father in the name of our Lord Jesus Christ; (KJV).

We need to pray all the time.

Ephesians 6:18

Praying always with all prayer and supplication in the Spirit, and watching thereunto with all perseverance and supplication for all saints; (KJV).

We need to pray with confidence—in accordance with God's will.

1 John 5:14

And this is the confidence that we have in him, that, if we ask any thing according to his will, he heareth us: (KJV).

We need to pray with thanksgiving.

1 Thessalonians 5:18

In every thing give thanks: for this is the will of God in Christ Jesus concerning you (KJV).

We need to pray with sincerity.

Ephesians 6:24

Grace be with all them that love our Lord Jesus Christ in sincerity. Amen (KJV).

We need to pray without doubting.

James 1:6

But he must ask in faith, without any doubts, for the one who has doubts is like a wave of the sea that is driven and tossed by the wind (ISV).

We need to pray boldly.

Hebrews 4:16

Let us therefore draw near with boldness unto the throne of grace, that we may receive mercy, and may find grace to help us in time of need (ASV).

We need to pray with the right motives.

James 4:3

Ye ask, and receive not, because ye ask amiss, that ye may spend it in your pleasures (ASV).

We need to pray according to God's will.

1 John 5:14, 15

14 And this is the boldness which we have toward him, that, if we ask anything according to his will, he heareth us:

15 and if we know that he heareth us whatsoever we ask, we know that we have the petitions which we have asked of him (ASV).

Prayer will give us peace.

Philippians 4:6, 7

6 In nothing be anxious; but in everything by prayer and supplication with thanksgiving let your requests be made known unto God.

⁷ And the peace of God, which passeth all understanding, shall guard your hearts and your thoughts in Christ Jesus (ASV).

Prayer accomplishes much.

James 5:16-18

¹⁶ Confess therefore your sins one to another, and pray one for another, that ye may be healed. The supplication of a righteous man availeth much in its working.

¹⁷ Elijah was a man of like passions with us, and he prayed fervently that it might not rain; and it rained not on the earth for three years and six months.

¹⁸ And he prayed again; and the heaven gave rain, and the earth brought forth her fruit (ASV).

We need to pray to gain strength and overcome temptation.

Matthew 26:41

Watch and pray, that ye enter not into temptation: the spirit indeed is willing, but the flesh is weak (ASV).

The Holy Spirit helps us to pray.

Ephesians 6:18

praying at all times in the Spirit, with all prayer and supplication. To that end, keep alert with all perseverance, making supplication for all the saints, (ESV).

Romans 8:26, 27

²⁶ Likewise the Spirit helps us in our weakness. For we do not know what to pray for as we ought, but the Spirit himself intercedes for us with groanings too deep for words.

²⁷ And he who searches hearts knows what is the mind of the Spirit, because the Spirit intercedes for the saints according to the will of God (ESV).

4. Worship & Praise

Definition:

1. To adore; to pay divine honors to; to reverence with supreme respect and veneration.
2. The act of expressing approval or admiration; the offering of grateful homage in words or song to God.

Premise:

Worship is immeasurably important because God is immeasurably worthy. The purpose of worship is to praise, glorify, honor, exalt, and please God. Our worship must show our adoration and loyalty to God for His love, grace, and mercy in providing us a way to escape the eternal consequences of sin. Worship is reserved for God alone for Who He is, and praise is a joyful thanksgiving to God for what He has done.

Conclusion:

We can have a fulfilling relationship with God and experience genuine love, worship, service, and fellowship with Him through Jesus Christ. As He calls us to worship Him in spirit and in truth, let's understand that worship is paying deep, sincere love and adoration with total surrender, out of respect for the God Who loves us, created us, and saved us.

Proof Texts:

Worship is an encounter with the living and holy God.

Exodus 3:1-6

¹ Now Moses was keeping the flock of Jethro his father-in-law, the priest of Midian: and he led the flock to the back of the wilderness, and came to the mountain of God, unto Horeb.

² And the angel of Jehovah appeared unto him in a flame of fire out of the midst of a bush: and he looked, and, behold, the bush burned with fire, and the bush was not consumed.

³ And Moses said, I will turn aside now, and see this great sight, why the bush is not burnt.

4 And when Jehovah saw that he turned aside to see, God called unto him out of the midst of the bush, and said, Moses, Moses. And he said, Here am I.

5 And he said, Draw not nigh hither: put off thy shoes from off thy feet, for the place whereon thou standest is holy ground.

6 Moreover he said, I am the God of thy father, the God of Abraham, the God of Isaac, and the God of Jacob. And Moses hid his face; for he was afraid to look upon God (ASV).

Worship is reserved for God alone.

Exodus 34:14

for thou shalt worship no other god: for Jehovah, whose name is Jealous, is a jealous God: (ASV).

Luke 4:8

And Jesus answered and said unto him, It is written, Thou shalt worship the Lord thy God, and him only shalt thou serve (ASV).

In worship, we ascribe to the Lord the glory due to Him.

Psalm 29:1, 2

1 A Psalm of David. Ascribe unto Jehovah, O ye sons of the mighty, Ascribe unto Jehovah glory and strength.

2 Ascribe unto Jehovah the glory due unto his name; Worship Jehovah in holy array (ASV).

We worship because of Christ's sacrifice on our behalf.

Hebrews 10:1-10

1 For the law having a shadow of the good things to come, not the very image of the things, can never with the same sacrifices year by year, which they offer continually, make perfect them that draw nigh.

2 Else would they not have ceased to be offered? because the worshippers, having been once cleansed, would have had no more consciousness of sins.

3 But in those sacrifices there is a remembrance made of sins year by year.

4 For it is impossible that the blood of bulls and goats should take away sins.

5 Wherefore when he cometh into the world, he saith, Sacrifice and offering thou wouldest not, But a body didst thou prepare for me;

6 In whole burnt offerings and sacrifices for sin thou hadst no pleasure:

7 Then said I, Lo, I am come (In the roll of the book it is written of me) To do thy will, O God.

8 Saying above, Sacrifices and offerings and whole burnt offerings and sacrifices for sin thou wouldest not, neither hadst pleasure therein (the which are offered according to the law),

9 then hath he said, Lo, I am come to do thy will. He taketh away the first, that he may establish the second.

10 By which will we have been sanctified through the offering of the body of Jesus Christ once for all (ASV).

We worship with reverence for God.

Hebrews 12:28

Wherefore, receiving a kingdom that cannot be shaken, let us have grace, whereby we may offer service well- pleasing to God with reverence and awe: (ASV).

When we draw near to God, He draws near to us.

James 4:8

Come close to God, and he will come close to you. Cleanse your hands, you sinners, and purify your hearts, you double-minded (ISV).

God calls us to true worship.

John 4:21-24

21 Jesus saith unto her, Woman, believe me, the hour cometh, when ye shall neither in this mountain, nor yet at Jerusalem, worship the Father.

22 Ye worship ye know not what: we know what we worship: for salvation is of the Jews.

23 But the hour cometh, and now is, when the true worshippers shall worship the Father in spirit and in truth: for the Father seeketh such to worship him.

24 God is a Spirit: and they that worship him must worship him in spirit and in truth (KJV).

Psalm 8:1

O Jehovah, our Lord, How excellent is thy name in all the earth, Who hast set thy glory upon the heavens! (ASV).

Psalm 95:6

Oh come, let us worship and bow down; Let us kneel before Jehovah our Maker: (ASV).

Psalm 99:5

Exalt ye Jehovah our God, And worship at his footstool: Holy is he (ASV).

God gives us reasons for worship.

Deuteronomy 12:5-7

5 But unto the place which Jehovah your God shall choose out of all your tribes, to put his name there, even unto his habitation shall ye seek, and thither thou shalt come;

6 and thither ye shall bring your burnt-offerings, and your sacrifices, and your tithes, and the heave-offering of your hand, and your vows, and your freewill-offerings, and the firstlings of your herd and of your flock:

7 and there ye shall eat before Jehovah your God, and ye shall rejoice in all that ye put your hand unto, ye and your households, wherein Jehovah thy God hath blessed thee (ASV).

Philippians 2:9-11

9 Wherefore also God highly exalted him, and gave unto him the name which is above every name;

10 that in the name of Jesus every knee should bow, of things in heaven and things on earth and things under the earth,

11 and that every tongue should confess that Jesus Christ is Lord, to the glory of God the Father (ASV).

Revelation 5:9

And they sung a new song, saying, Thou art worthy to take the book, and to open the seals thereof: for thou wast slain, and hast redeemed us to God by thy blood out of every kindred, and tongue, and people, and nation; (KJV).

Revelation 4:11

Thou art worthy, O Lord, to receive glory and honour and power: for thou hast created all things, and for thy pleasure they are and were created (KJV).

Colossians 1:16

For by him were all things created, that are in heaven, and that are in earth, visible and invisible, whether they be thrones, or dominions, or principalities, or powers: all things were created by him, and for him: (KJV).

God gives us examples of worship.

Exodus 33:9, 10

⁹ And it came to pass, as Moses entered into the tabernacle, the cloudy pillar descended, and stood at the door of the tabernacle, and the LORD talked with Moses.

¹⁰ And all the people saw the cloudy pillar stand at the tabernacle door: and all the people rose up and worshipped, every man in his tent door (KJV).

Psalm 100:4

Enter into his gates with thanksgiving, and into his courts with praise: be thankful unto him, and bless his name (KJV).

Romans 12:1, 2

¹ I beseech you therefore, brethren, by the mercies of God, that ye present your bodies a living sacrifice, holy, acceptable unto God, which is your reasonable service.

² And be not conformed to this world: but be ye transformed by the renewing of your mind, that ye may prove what is that good, and acceptable, and perfect, will of God (KJV).

Galatians 2:20

I am crucified with Christ: nevertheless I live; yet not I, but Christ liveth in me: and the life which I now live in the flesh I live by the faith of the Son of God, who loved me, and gave himself for me (KJV).

Hebrews 5:7

Who in the days of his flesh, when he had offered up prayers and supplications with strong crying and tears unto him that was able to save him from death, and was heard in that he feared; (KJV).

We are to worship God in song: Praise is interwoven with worship.

Exodus 15:20, 21

20 And Miriam the prophetess, the sister of Aaron, took a timbrel in her hand; and all the women went out after her with timbrels and with dances.

21 And Miriam answered them, Sing ye to the LORD, for he hath triumphed gloriously; the horse and his rider hath he thrown into the sea (KJV).

Psalm 59:16

But I will sing of thy power; yea, I will sing aloud of thy mercy in the morning: for thou hast been my defence and refuge in the day of my trouble (KJV).

Psalm 63:3, 4

3 Because thy lovingkindness is better than life, my lips shall praise thee.

4 Thus will I bless thee while I live: I will lift up my hands in thy name (KJV).

Psalm 66:3, 4

3 Say unto God, How terrible art thou in thy works! through the greatness of thy power shall thine enemies submit themselves unto thee.

4 All the earth shall worship thee, and shall sing unto thee; they shall sing to thy name. Selah (KJV).

Psalm 150 (This Psalm has only 6 verses.)

1 Praise ye the LORD. Praise God in his sanctuary: praise him in the firmament of his power.

2 Praise him for his mighty acts: praise him according to his excellent greatness.

3 Praise him with the sound of the trumpet: praise him with the psaltery and harp.

4 Praise him with the timbrel and dance: praise him with stringed instruments and organs.

5 Praise him upon the loud cymbals: praise him upon the high sounding cymbals.

6 Let every thing that hath breath praise the LORD. Praise ye the LORD (KJV).

Psalm 107:8, 9

8 Oh that men would praise the LORD for his goodness, and for his wonderful works to the children of men!

9 For he satisfieth the longing soul, and filleth the hungry soul with goodness (KJV).

Psalm 106:1, 2

1 Praise ye the LORD. O give thanks unto the LORD; for he is good: for his mercy endureth for ever.

2 Who can utter the mighty acts of the LORD? who can shew forth all his praise? (KJV).

1 Thessalonians 5:16-18

16 Rejoice evermore.

17 Pray without ceasing.

18 In every thing give thanks: for this is the will of God in Christ Jesus concerning you (KJV).

Luke 19:38

Saying, Blessed be the King that cometh in the name of the Lord: peace in heaven, and glory in the highest (KJV).

Christ is worthy of praise.

Revelation 5:12

They sang with a loud voice, "Worthy is the lamb who was slaughtered to receive power, wealth, wisdom, strength, honor, glory, and praise!" (ISV).

The Holy Spirit helps us to worship.

Philippians 3:3

For we are the circumcision, who worship by the Spirit of God and glory in Christ Jesus and put no confidence in the flesh—*(ESV)*.

God has shown us in His Word that He loves us and that He is reliable, trustworthy, forgiving, gracious, merciful, and steadfast. We are thankful to God because He is faithful and supplies our every need, and He is worthy to be worshiped.

5. Fellowship

Definition:

Fellowship is a relationship of unity among believers that expresses itself in co-participation with Christ and one another in accomplishing God's will on Earth. It is the building up, encouraging, and equipping of the body of Christ by the body of Christ.

Premise:

Fellowship is immensely important to the believer because it reinforces Christ in our mind, heart, and soul; and it helps us to focus on His desires and goals for us. Christian fellowship also sharpens one another's faith and encourages one another to exercise our faith in love and good works to God's glory. The word translated *"fellowship"* in the Greek is the word *"koinonia,"* and it means essentially to partner together for the mutual benefit of those involved. Christian fellowship exists because God has enabled it by His love, mercy, grace, and forgiveness. Those who believe the Gospel message are united in one Spirit through Jesus Christ, and that unity is the basis of our fellowship. This relationship is described by Jesus to His followers in His prayer for them in the Gospel of John chapter seventeen.

Conclusion:

True Christian fellowship can only occur within the body of Christ. Every believer needs to be in fellowship with other believers. Scripture should control every thought, word, and deed in fellowship as Christians are united in fellowship in Jesus Christ to one another by common beliefs, purposes, and goals. These beliefs, purposes, and goals are found at one source—the Bible. Understand the Bible. We need to study it and pray for guidance and direction from the Holy Spirit as we live this life with Him and for Him, loving one another and longing for the time when we will be with Christ forever in our true home—Heaven!

Proof Texts:

As Christians we have fellowship with the Father and the Son.

1 John 1:3

that which we have seen and heard we proclaim also to you, so that you too may have fellowship with us; and indeed our fellowship is with the Father and with his Son Jesus Christ (ESV).

1 Corinthians 1:9

God is faithful, by whom ye were called unto the fellowship of his Son Jesus Christ our Lord (KJV).

As Christians we have fellowship with the Holy Spirit.

2 Corinthians 13:14

The grace of the Lord Jesus Christ, and the love of God, and the communion of the Holy Ghost, be with you all. Amen (KJV).

As Christians we have fellowship with one another.

1 John 1:7

But if we walk in the light, as he is in the light, we have fellowship one with another, and the blood of Jesus Christ his Son cleanseth us from all sin (KJV).

Fellowship must have love, patience, and peace.

Ephesians 4:1-3

¹ I therefore, a prisoner for the Lord, urge you to walk in a manner worthy of the calling to which you have been called,

² with all humility and gentleness, with patience, bearing with one another in love,

³ eager to maintain the unity of the Spirit in the bond of peace (ESV).

Fellowship must have encouragement, compassion, sympathy, and love in unity.

Philippians 2:1, 2

¹ Therefore, if there is any encouragement in Christ, if there is any comfort of love, if there is any fellowship in the Spirit, if there is any compassion and sympathy,

² then fill me with joy by having the same attitude, sharing the same love, being united in spirit, and keeping one purpose in mind (ISV).

Fellowship must not have divisions.

1 Corinthians 1:10

Brothers, I urge all of you in the name of our Lord Jesus Christ to be in agreement and not to have divisions among you, so that you may be perfectly united in your understanding and opinions (ISV).

We are not to neglect having fellowship with other believers.

Hebrews 10:24, 25

²⁴ And let us consider one another to provoke unto love and to good works:

²⁵ Not forsaking the assembling of ourselves together, as the manner of some is; but exhorting one another: and so much the more, as ye see the day approaching (KJV).

Hebrews 13:1

Let brotherly love continue (ISV).

We are made perfect in one.

John 17:23

I in them, and thou in me, that they may be made perfect in one; and that the world may know that thou hast sent me, and hast loved them, as thou hast loved me (KJV).

Our fellowship is with genuine believers.

1 John 1:6, 7

⁶ If we say that we have fellowship with him, and walk in darkness, we lie, and do not the truth:

7 But if we walk in the light, as he is in the light, we have fellowship one with another, and the blood of Jesus Christ his Son cleanseth us from all sin (KJV).

2 Corinthians 6:14

Be ye not unequally yoked together with unbelievers: for what fellowship hath righteousness with unrighteousness? and what communion hath light with darkness? (KJV).

We must continue in fellowship.

Acts 2:42, 44

42 And they continued steadfastly in the apostles' doctrine and fellowship, and in breaking of bread, and in prayers.

44 And all that believed were together, and had all things common; (KJV).

We must be hospitable and loving in fellowship.

1 Peter 4:9

Use hospitality one to another without grudging (KJV).

Romans 12:10

Be kindly affectioned one to another with brotherly love; in honour preferring one another; (KJV).

We must love each other intensely and sincerely with a pure heart.

1 Peter 1:22

Now that you have obeyed the truth and have purified your souls to love your brothers sincerely, you must love one another intensely and with a pure heart (ISV).

We must serve one another in love.

Galatians 5:13

For you, brothers, were called to freedom. Only do not turn your freedom into an opportunity to gratify your flesh, but through love make it your habit to serve one another (ISV).

Fellowship must be kind, forgiving, and good.

Ephesians 4:32

And be ye kind one to another, tenderhearted, forgiving one another, even as God for Christ's sake hath forgiven you (KJV).

Galatians 6:10

So then, as we have opportunity, let us do good to everyone, and especially to those who are of the household of faith (ESV).

Scripture should control every thought, word, and deed in fellowship.

Colossians 3:16

Let the word of Christ dwell in you richly in all wisdom; teaching and admonishing one another in psalms and hymns and spiritual songs, singing with grace in your hearts to the Lord (KJV).

Christian fellowship has unity in Christ.

John 17:22, 23

22 And the glory which thou gavest me I have given them; that they may be one, even as we are one:

23 I in them, and thou in me, that they may be made perfect in one; and that the world may know that thou hast sent me, and hast loved them, as thou hast loved me (KJV).

We must bear one another's burdens.

Galatians 6:2

Bear one another's burdens, and so fulfill the law of Christ (ESV).

Our love comes from the Holy Spirit.

1 John 4:11-13

11 Beloved, if God so loved us, we also ought to love one another.

12 No one has ever seen God; if we love one another, God abides in us and his love is perfected in us.

13 By this we know that we abide in him and he in us, because he has given us of his Spirit (ESV).

We must exhort one another in fellowship.

Hebrews 3:13

But exhort one another every day, as long as it is called "today," that none of you may be hardened by the deceitfulness of sin (ESV).

The Body of Christ is to work together.

Romans 12:4-6

⁴ For as in one body we have many members, and the members do not all have the same function,

⁵ so we, though many, are one body in Christ, and individually members one of another.

⁶ Having gifts that differ according to the grace given to us, let us use them: if prophecy, in proportion to our faith; (ESV).

Ephesians 4:15, 16

¹⁵ Rather, speaking the truth in love, we are to grow up in every way into him who is the head, into Christ,

¹⁶ from whom the whole body, joined and held together by every joint with which it is equipped, when each part is working properly, makes the body grow so that it builds itself up in love (ESV).

Ephesians 4:4-6

⁴ There is one body and one Spirit—just as you were called to the one hope that belongs to your call—

⁵ one Lord, one faith, one baptism,

⁶ one God and Father of all, who is over all and through all and in all (ESV).

6. Evangelism

Definition:

1. To bring the Good News message; to proclaim the Gospel of Jesus Christ to those who have never heard; to announce that Gospel to others.
2. To witness.

Premise:

Evangelism is significantly important because it reveals God's plan of redemption to a lost and dying world. Since God has saved us and called us to tell others the Gospel, do not be ashamed to share the Gospel. Instead, share it with gentleness and respect to anyone who asks about your hope as you completely rely on God to reach the heart and mind of the lost. Preaching the Gospel is not about intellectual superiority: it is about Jesus Christ and His death, burial, and resurrection.

Conclusion:

We must remember that every act of evangelism is meant to be a demonstration of the Holy Spirit's power, not our own. The Gospel is a message of hope, and we need to always be ready to give an answer for that hope, and we must remember only Christ can offer real, lasting hope and change a person's heart. Salvation is a work and gift of the Holy Spirit. We must allow God's love to work through us if we are going to effectively share the Gospel to the lost and dying world. Allowing God to do this through us must be priority.

Proof Texts:

We are God's messengers.

Isaiah 43:10, 11

10 Ye are my witnesses, saith Jehovah, and my servant whom I have chosen; that ye may know and believe me, and understand that I am he: before me there was no God formed, neither shall there be after me.

11 I, even I, am Jehovah; and besides me there is no saviour (ASV).

Christians bring light to a spiritually dark world.

Matthew 5:14-16

14 Ye are the light of the world. A city set on a hill cannot be hid.

15 Neither do men light a lamp, and put it under the bushel, but on the stand; and it shineth unto all that are in the house.

16 Even so let your light shine before men; that they may see your good works, and glorify your Father who is in heaven (ASV).

Jesus made salvation available to all people.

John 3:16-18

16 For this is how God loved the world: He gave his unique Son so that everyone who believes in him might not perish but have eternal life.

17 For God sent the Son into the world, not to condemn the world, but that the world might be saved through him.

18 Whoever believes in him is not condemned, but whoever does not believe has already been condemned, because he has not believed in the name of God's unique Son (ISV).

We need to be bold in our evangelism.

Matthew 10:33

But whosoever shall deny me before men, him will I also deny before my Father which is in heaven (KJV).

Ephesians 6:19, 20

19 Pray also for me, so that, when I open my mouth, the right words will be given to me. Then I will boldly make known the secret of the gospel,

20 for whose sake I am an ambassador in chains, desiring to declare it as boldly as I should (ISV).

Jesus sent His followers to make disciples.

Matthew 28:18-20

18 Then Jesus came up and said to them, "All authority in heaven and on earth has been given to me.

19 Therefore, as you go, disciple all the nations, baptizing them in the name of the Father, and of the Son, and of the Holy Spirit,

20 teaching them to obey all that I have commanded you. And remember, I am with you each and every day until the end of the age"(ISV).

The Holy Spirit gives us power to evangelize.

Acts 1:8

But ye shall receive power, after that the Holy Ghost is come upon you: and ye shall be witnesses unto me both in Jerusalem, and in all Judaea, and in Samaria, and unto the uttermost part of the earth (KJV).

The Holy Spirit gives power and conviction in the Gospel.

1 Thessalonians 1:5

because our gospel came to you not only in word, but also in power and in the Holy Spirit and with full conviction. You know what kind of men we proved to be (ESV).

Bringing the Good News of Christ is a wonderful privilege.

Isaiah 52:7

How beautiful upon the mountains are the feet of him who brings good news, who publishes peace, who brings good news of happiness, who publishes salvation, who says to Zion, "Your God reigns"(ESV).

God's message will accomplish what He desires wherever it is spoken.

Isaiah 55:10, 11

¹⁰ For as the rain cometh down, and the snow from heaven, and returneth not thither, but watereth the earth, and maketh it bring forth and bud, that it may give seed to the sower, and bread to the eater:

¹¹ So shall my word be that goeth forth out of my mouth: it shall not return unto me void, but it shall accomplish that which I please, and it shall prosper in the thing whereto I sent it (KJV).

God holds us accountable for avoiding a chance to witness for Him.

Ezekiel 3:18, 19

¹⁸ If I say to the wicked, "You shall surely die," and you give him no warning, nor speak to warn the wicked from his wicked way, in order to save his life, that wicked person shall die for his iniquity, but his blood I will require at your hand. ¹⁹ But if you warn the wicked, and he does not turn from his wickedness, or from his wicked way, he shall die for his iniquity, but you will have delivered your soul (ESV).

We Christians need to let our light shine.

Matthew 5:14-16

14 Ye are the light of the world. A city that is set on an hill cannot be hid.

15 Neither do men light a candle, and put it under a bushel, but on a candlestick; and it giveth light unto all that are in the house.

16 Let your light so shine before men, that they may see your good works, and glorify your Father which is in heaven (KJV).

Jesus commanded all believers to witness.

Matthew 28:16-20

18 Then Jesus came up and said to them, "All authority in heaven and on earth has been given to me.

19 Therefore, as you go, disciple all the nations, baptizing them in the name of the Father, and of the Son, and of the Holy Spirit,

20 teaching them to obey all that I have commanded you. And remember, I am with you each and every day until the end of the age" (ISV).

If we acknowledge Jesus before people, Jesus will acknowledge us.

Luke 12:8, 9

8 Also I say unto you, Whosoever shall confess me before men, him shall the Son of man also confess before the angels of God:

9 But he that denieth me before men shall be denied before the angels of God (KJV).

Christians are called to spread the Gospel across the world.

Acts 1:8

But ye shall receive power, after that the Holy Ghost is come upon you: and ye shall be witnesses unto me both in Jerusalem, and in all Judaea, and in Samaria, and unto the uttermost part of the earth (KJV).

We plant the seed of faith, but only God makes it grow.

1 Corinthians 3:5, 6

5 What then is Apollos? What is Paul? Servants through whom you believed, as the Lord assigned to each.

6 I planted, Apollos watered, but God gave the growth (ESV).

1 Corinthians 3:7-9

7 So neither he who plants nor he who waters is anything, but only God who gives the growth.

8 He who plants and he who waters are one, and each will receive his wages according to his labor.

9 For we are God's fellow workers. You are God's field, God's building (ESV).

God has entrusted us with the message we need to share with others.

2 Corinthians 5:18-21

18 And all things are of God, who hath reconciled us to himself by Jesus Christ, and hath given to us the ministry of reconciliation;

19 To wit, that God was in Christ, reconciling the world unto himself, not imputing their trespasses unto them; and hath committed unto us the word of reconciliation.

20 Now then we are ambassadors for Christ, as though God did beseech you by us: we pray you in Christ's stead, be ye reconciled to God.

21 For he hath made him to be sin for us, who knew no sin; that we might be made the righteousness of God in him (KJV).

We must always be ready to tell what God has done for us.

1 Peter 3:15

but in your hearts honor Christ the Lord as holy, always being prepared to make a defense to anyone who asks you for a reason for the hope that is in you; yet do it with gentleness and respect, (ESV).

We must not be ashamed of the Gospel.

Romans 1:16

For I am not ashamed of the gospel of Christ: for it is the power of God unto salvation to every one that believeth; to the Jew first, and also to the Greek (KJV).

2 Timothy 1:7-9

7 For God hath not given us the spirit of fear; but of power, and of love, and of a sound mind.

8 Be not thou therefore ashamed of the testimony of our Lord, nor of me his prisoner: but be thou partaker of the afflictions of the gospel according to the power of God;

9 Who hath saved us, and called us with an holy calling, not according to our works, but according to his own purpose and grace, which was given us in Christ Jesus before the world began, (KJV).

Evangelism is important to Jesus.

Luke 10:1, 2

1 After these things the Lord appointed other seventy also, and sent them two and two before his face into every city and place, whither he himself would come.

2 Therefore said he unto them, The harvest truly is great, but the labourers are few: pray ye therefore the Lord of the harvest, that he would send forth labourers into his harvest (KJV).

Matthew 9:37, 38

37 Then saith he unto his disciples, The harvest truly is plenteous, but the labourers are few;

38 Pray ye therefore the Lord of the harvest, that he will send forth labourers into his harvest (KJV).

Matthew 28:19, 20

19 Go ye therefore, and teach all nations, baptizing them in the name of the Father, and of the Son, and of the Holy Ghost:

20 Teaching them to observe all things whatsoever I have commanded you: and, lo, I am with you always, even unto the end of the world. Amen (KJV).

Evangelism is about Christ, not our intellectual superiority.

1 Corinthians 2:1-5

1 And I, brethren, when I came to you, came not with excellency of speech or of wisdom, declaring unto you the testimony of God.

2 For I determined not to know any thing among you, save Jesus Christ, and him crucified.

3 And I was with you in weakness, and in fear, and in much trembling.

4 And my speech and my preaching was not with enticing words of man's wisdom, but in demonstration of the Spirit and of power:

5 That your faith should not stand in the wisdom of men, but in the power of God (KJV).

7. Discipleship

Definition:

A disciple is a believer and follower of Jesus Christ who accepts and assists in the spreading of the Gospel as well as learning and obeying His teachings.

Premise:

Discipleship is extraordinarily important because it is the process by which followers of the Lord Jesus Christ grow in the Lord Jesus Christ; and they do so in obedience and understanding as they are assisted by the Word of God and the Holy Spirit Who resides in their heart.

Conclusion:

There are ten main criteria found in the Bible that a disciple needs to follow.

1. Deny yourself.	6. Study the Bible.
2. Carry your cross.	7. Love others.
3. Abide in Christ.	8. Make disciples.
4. Be baptized.	9. Share the Gospel.
5. Pray daily.	10. Obey God.

Proof Texts:

Disciples are to evangelize and make disciples.

Matthew 28:19, 20

19 Go therefore and make disciples of all nations, baptizing them in the name of the Father and of the Son and of the Holy Spirit,

²⁰ *teaching them to observe all that I have commanded you. And behold, I am with you always, to the end of the age (ESV).*

We disciples are known by our love.

John 13:35

By this all people will know that you are my disciples, if you have love for one another (ESV).

Disciples help other people grow.

Acts 14:21, 22

21 When they had preached the gospel to that city and had made many disciples, they returned to Lystra and to Iconium and to Antioch,

22 strengthening the souls of the disciples, encouraging them to continue in the faith, and saying that through many tribulations we must enter the kingdom of God (ESV).

Disciples of Christ are the light of the world.

Matthew 5:14-16

¹⁴ You are the light of the world. A city set on a hill cannot be hidden.

¹⁵ Nor do people light a lamp and put it under a basket, but on a stand, and it gives light to all in the house.

¹⁶ In the same way, let your light shine before others, so that they may see your good works and give glory to your Father who is in heaven (ESV).

Ephesians 5:8

For you were once darkness, but now you are light in the Lord; walk as children of light (ESV).

We disciples must bear our cross.

Luke 14:27

Whoever does not bear his own cross and come after me cannot be my disciple (ESV).

We disciples must deny ourselves, carry our cross, and follow Christ.

Matthew 16:24

Then Jesus told his disciples, "If anyone would come after me, let him deny himself and take up his cross and follow me" (ESV).

Disciples must be faithful people.

2 Timothy 2:2

and what you have heard from me in the presence of many witnesses entrust to faithful men who will be able to teach others also (ESV).

Disciples must equip and edify the Body of Christ.

Ephesians 4:12

to equip the saints for the work of ministry, for building up the body of Christ, (ESV).

Disciples must abide in Christ's Word.

John 8: 31, 32

³¹ So Jesus said to the Jews who had believed in him, "If you abide in my word, you are truly my disciples,

³² And you shall know the truth, and the truth shall make you free" (ESV).

Disciples must bear fruit.

John 15:2

Every branch in me that does not bear fruit he takes away, and every branch that does bear fruit he prunes, that it may bear more fruit (ESV).

Disciples must baptize others.

Matthew 28:19

¹⁹ Therefore, as you go, disciple all the nations, baptizing them in the name of the Father, and of the Son, and of the Holy Spirit (ISV),

Disciples must teach others.

Matthew 28:20

²⁰ teaching them to obey all that I have commanded you. And remember, I am with you each and every day until the end of the age (ISV).

Disciples must love one another.

John 13:34, 35

34 *A new commandment I give to you, that you love one another: just as I have loved you, you also are to love one another.*

35 *By this all shall know that you are My disciples, if you have love toward one another (ESV).*

Disciples are not above Christ.

Luke 6:40

A disciple is not above his teacher, but everyone when he is fully trained will be like his teacher (ESV).

We disciples must forsake all that we have.

Luke 14:33

So therefore, any one of you who does not renounce all that he has cannot be my disciple (ESV).

Disciples must speak sound doctrine.

Titus 2:1

But as for you, teach what accords with sound doctrine (ESV).

Disciples are ambassadors for Christ.

2 Corinthians 5:20

Therefore, we are ambassadors for Christ, God making his appeal through us. We implore you on behalf of Christ, be reconciled to God (ESV).

Disciples are both of men and women.

Acts 5:14

and more believing ones were added to the Lord, multitudes both of men and women; (ESV).

Acts 8:12

But when they believed Philip as he preached good news about the kingdom of God and the name of Jesus Christ, they were baptized, both men and women (ESV).

Acts 17:12

Therefore many of them believed, and quite a few of honorable Greek women and men (ESV).

8. Baptism

Definition:

Baptism signifies

1. A confession of faith in Christ;
2. A cleansing or washing of the soul from sin;
3. A death to sin and a new life in righteousness; and
4. The death, burial, and resurrection of Jesus Christ.

Premise:

Baptism symbolizes the death, burial, and resurrection of Christ and our new beginning in Christ, set apart from a lost and dying world. Baptism is important because it is a direct, obedient act of a disciple of Jesus Christ after his or her conversion — after a person believes and trusts in Christ as Savior and Lord.

Conclusion:

The symbol of baptism testifies to a lost and dying world that a disciple of Christ is washed, sanctified, and justified in the name of the Lord Jesus Christ. Water baptism is a public profession of a person's repentance and faith in Jesus Christ. It could be said that baptism is an outward testimony of the inward work of God in the heart, mind, and soul of a person who was lost and now is found in Christ.

Proof Texts:

Baptism signifies repentance.

Acts 2:38

Then Peter said unto them, Repent, and be baptized every one of you in the name of Jesus Christ for the remission of sins, and ye shall receive the gift of the Holy Ghost (KJV).

Baptism is for followers of Christ.

Romans 6:1-6

¹ What should we say, then? Should we go on sinning so that grace may increase?

2 Of course not! How can we who died as far as sin is concerned go on living in it?

3 Or don't you know that all of us who were baptized into union with Christ Jesus were baptized into his death?

4 Therefore, through baptism we were buried with him into his death so that, just as Christ was raised from the dead by the Father's glory, we too may live an entirely new life.

5 For if we have become united with him in a death like his, we will certainly also be united with him in a resurrection like his.

6 We know that our old selves were crucified with him so that our sinful bodies might be rendered powerless and we might no longer be slaves to sin (ISV).

Matthew 28:19

Go therefore and make disciples of all nations, baptizing them in the name of the Father and of the Son and of the Holy Spirit, (ESV).

Acts 2:38

Then Peter said unto them, Repent, and be baptized every one of you in the name of Jesus Christ for the remission of sins, and ye shall receive the gift of the Holy Ghost (KJV).

Ephesians 4:5

One Lord, one faith, one baptism, (KJV).

Jesus was baptized.

Mark 1:9

In those days Jesus came from Nazareth of Galilee and was baptized by John in the Jordan.

Baptism is a direct, obedient act of a believer.

Acts 8:12, 35-38

8:12 But when Philip proclaimed the good news of the kingdom of God and of the name of Jesus Christ, men and women believed and were baptized.

35 Then Philip opened his mouth and, starting from this Scripture, told him the good news about Jesus.

36 As they were going along the road, they came to some water. The eunuch said, "Look, there's some water. What keeps me from being baptized?"

37 Philip said, "If you believe with all your heart, you may." He replied, "I believe that Jesus Christ is the Son of God."

38 So he ordered the chariot to stop, and Philip and the eunuch both went down into the water, and Philip baptized him (ISV).

Acts 2:38

Then Peter said unto them, Repent, and be baptized every one of you in the name of Jesus Christ for the remission of sins, and ye shall receive the gift of the Holy Ghost (KJV).

Entire families were baptized.

Acts 16:33, 34

33 At that hour of the night he took them and washed their wounds. Then he and his entire family were baptized immediately. And when she was baptized, and her household,.... (KJV).

34 He brought them upstairs into his house and set food before them, and he and everyone in his house were thrilled to be believers in God (ISV).

Baptism symbolizes the death, burial, and resurrection of Christ.

Colossians 2:12

Buried with him in baptism, wherein also ye are risen with him through the faith of the operation of God, who hath raised him from the dead (KJV).

Romans 6:3-8

3 Or don't you know that all of us who were baptized into union with Christ Jesus were baptized into his death?

4 Therefore, through baptism we were buried with him into his death so that, just as Christ was raised from the dead by the Father's glory, we too may live an entirely new life.

5 For if we have become united with him in a death like his, we will certainly also be united with him in a resurrection like his.

6 We know that our old selves were crucified with him so that our sinful bodies might be rendered powerless and we might no longer be slaves to sin.

7 For the person who has died has been freed from sin.

8 Now if we have died with Christ, we believe that we will also live with him, (ISV).

Baptism also represents the passing of the old life to the new life.

2 Corinthians 5:17

Therefore if any man be in Christ, he is a new creature: old things are passed away; behold, all things are become new (KJV).

Baptism refers to clothing oneself with Christ.

Galatians 3:27

For as many of you as have been baptized into Christ have put on Christ (KJV).

Baptism is a symbol of our sanctification and justification through Jesus Christ.

1 Corinthians 6:11

And such were some of you: but ye are washed, but ye are sanctified, but ye are justified in the name of the Lord Jesus, and by the Spirit of our God (KJV).

Baptism is important but not necessary for salvation.

Luke 23:39-43

39 Now one of the criminals hanging there kept insulting him, saying, "You are the Christ, aren't you? Save yourself and us!"

40 But the other one rebuked him, saying, "Aren't you afraid of God, since you are suffering the same penalty?

41 We have been condemned justly, for we are getting what we deserve for our deeds, but this man has done nothing wrong."

42 Then he went on to say, "Jesus, remember me when you come into your kingdom!"

⁴³ Jesus said to him, "Truly I tell you, today you will be with me in Paradise" (ISV).

Luke 7:50

And he said to the woman, Thy faith hath saved thee; go in peace (KJV).

Paul was not sent to baptize, but to preach the Gospel.

1 Corinthians 1:17

For Christ sent me not to baptize, but to preach the gospel: not with wisdom of words, lest the cross of Christ should be made of none effect (KJV).

Paul baptized Crispus, Gaius, and the household of Stephanas.

1 Corinthians 1:14-16

¹⁴ I thank God that I baptized none of you, but Crispus and Gaius;

¹⁵ Lest any should say that I had baptized in mine own name.

¹⁶ And I baptized also the household of Stephanas: besides, I know not whether I baptized any other (KJV).

Paul gives an outline of the Gospel and never mentions baptism.

1 Corinthians 15:1-8

¹ Moreover, brethren, I declare unto you the gospel which I preached unto you, which also ye have received, and wherein ye stand;

² By which also ye are saved, if ye keep in memory what I preached unto you, unless ye have believed in vain.

³ For I delivered unto you first of all that which I also received, how that Christ died for our sins according to the scriptures;

⁴ And that he was buried, and that he rose again the third day according to the scriptures:

⁵ And that he was seen of Cephas, then of the twelve:

⁶ After that, he was seen of above five hundred brethren at once; of whom the greater part remain unto this present, but some are fallen asleep.

7 After that, he was seen of James; then of all the apostles.

8 And last of all he was seen of me also, as of one born out of due time (KJV).

People were saved and then baptized.

Acts 10:44-48

44 While Peter yet spake these words, the Holy Ghost fell on all them which heard the word.

45 And they of the circumcision which believed were astonished, as many as came with Peter, because that on the Gentiles also was poured out the gift of the Holy Ghost.

46 For they heard them speak with tongues, and magnify God. Then answered Peter,

47 Can any man forbid water, that these should not be baptized, which have received the Holy Ghost as well as we?

48 And he commanded them to be baptized in the name of the Lord. Then prayed they him to tarry certain days (KJV).

Salvation is achieved through faith in Christ alone.

Ephesians 2:8, 9

8 For by grace are ye saved through faith; and that not of yourselves: it is the gift of God:

9 Not of works, lest any man should boast (KJV).

Romans 3:22-24

22 Even the righteousness of God which is by faith of Jesus Christ unto all and upon all them that believe: for there is no difference:

23 For all have sinned, and come short of the glory of God;

24 Being justified freely by his grace through the redemption that is in Christ Jesus:(KJV).

Truth Charts

Truth Charts©   The goal of Truth Charts is to break down truth as it is found in Scripture to its lowest common denominator whereby making Biblical truth easy to understand and remember. Truth Charts© share the truth of God's Word simply. Truth Charts, Copyright ©2014 by David Wayne Meeker. All rights reserved.

TRUTH CHARTS

The first and most important actions a person can do in this life – according to the Bible – are these:

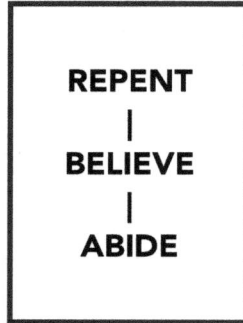

REPENT
|
BELIEVE
|
ABIDE

1. Repent

1 John 1:9

If we confess our sins, he is faithful and just to forgive us our sins, and to cleanse us from all unrighteousness (KJV).

2. Believe

John 3:16

For God so loved the world, that he gave his only begotten Son, that whosoever believeth in him should not perish, but have everlasting life (KJV).

3. Abide

John 15:4

Abide in me, and I in you. As the branch cannot bear fruit of itself, except it abide in the vine; no more can ye, except ye abide in me (KJV).

The most important thing we can do after we receive Christ is to share Christ according to the Bible.

```
┌─────────────────┐
│                 │
│    RECEIVE      │
│       |         │
│    SHARE        │
│                 │
└─────────────────┘
```

1. Receive

John 3:16

For God so loved the world, that he gave his only begotten Son, that whosoever believeth in him should not perish, but have everlasting life (KJV).

Romans 10:10

For the scripture saith, Whosoever believeth on him shall not be ashamed (KJV).

Romans 10:13

For whosoever shall call upon the name of the Lord shall be saved (KJV).

1 John 1:9

If we confess our sins, he is faithful and just to forgive us our sins, and to cleanse us from all unrighteousness (KJV).

2. Share

Matthew 28:19-20

19 "Therefore, as you go, disciple all the nations, baptizing them in the name of the Father, and of the Son, and of the Holy Spirit,

20 teaching them to obey all that I have commanded you. And remember, I am with you each and every day until the end of the age" (ISV).

1 Peter 3:15

But sanctify the Lord God in your hearts: and be ready always to give an answer to every man that asketh you a reason of the hope that is in you with meekness and fear: (KJV).

TC
TRUTH CHARTS

The Bible can be summed up in two categories: God wants to establish a relationship with us and improve our life through His Son Jesus Christ for both time and eternity.

ESTABLISH
|
IMPROVE

1. Establish

John 3:16

For God so loved the world, that he gave his only begotten Son, that whosoever believeth in him should not perish, but have everlasting life (KJV).

1 John 4:10

This is love: not that we have loved God, but that he loved us and sent his Son to be the atoning sacrifice for our sins (ISV).

2. Improve

Romans 6:23

For the wages of sin is death; but the gift of God is eternal life through Jesus Christ our Lord (KJV).

2 Corinthians 5:17

Therefore if any man be in Christ, he is a new creature: old things are passed away; behold, all things are become new (KJV).

TC
TRUTH
CHARTS

In His Word – God has revealed the cause, problem, and remedy for sin and death in this life.

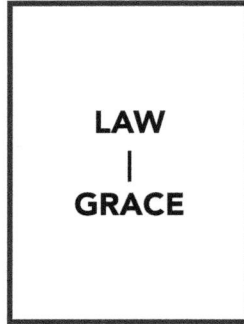

```
┌─────────────────────┐
│                     │
│                     │
│        LAW          │
│         |           │
│       GRACE         │
│                     │
│                     │
└─────────────────────┘
```

1. Law — Adam

Romans 5:12

Wherefore, as by one man sin entered into the world, and death by sin; and so death passed upon all men, for that all have sinned: (KJV).

2. Grace — Jesus

Romans 5:15

But not as the offence, so also is the free gift. For if through the offence of one many be dead, much more the grace of God, and the gift by grace, which is by one man, Jesus Christ, hath abounded unto many (KJV).

Romans 6:23

For the wages of sin is death; but the gift of God is eternal life through Jesus Christ our Lord (KJV).

Romans 8:2

For the law of the Spirit of life in Christ Jesus hath made me free from the law of sin and death (KJV).

TC **TRUTH CHARTS**

God has provided overwhelming evidence that the reliability and trustworthiness of His Word is proof of Divine origin and Divine inspiration.

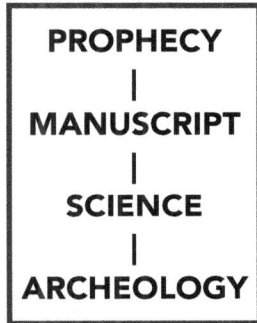

```
PROPHECY
   |
MANUSCRIPT
   |
SCIENCE
   |
ARCHEOLOGY
```

Recommended Reading:

The New Evidence that Demands a Verdict by Josh McDowell. Copyright ©1999 by Here's Life Publishers, Inc.

How to Receive Christ

Problem:

Scripture says that we have all sinned and fallen short of God's glorious plan. Sin separates us from God and leads to death and eternity in hell.

Proof Texts:

Romans 3:10

As it is written, "Not even one person is righteous" (ISV).

Romans 3:23

since all have sinned and continue to fall short of God's glory (ISV).

Romans 6:23

For the wages of sin is death, but the free gift of God is eternal life in union with Christ Jesus our Lord (ISV).

Solution:

God demonstrated His love to us by sending his Son to die for our sin.

Romans 5:8

but God shows his love for us in that while we were still sinners, Christ died for us (ESV).

Salvation comes from having trust and faith in Jesus Christ.

Proof Texts:

John 3:16

*For God so loved the world, that he gave his only begotten Son, that whoso-
ever believeth in him should not perish, but have everlasting life (KJV).*

Romans 10:13

For whosoever shall call upon the name of the Lord shall be saved (KJV).

1 John 1:9

*If we confess our sins, he is faithful and just to forgive us our sins, and to
cleanse us from all unrighteousness (KJV).*

Repent and believe in the Gospel.

Mark 1:15

*He said, "The time is now! The kingdom of God is near! Repent, and keep
believing the gospel!" (ISV).*

1 Corinthians 15:1-4

*¹ Now I'm making known to you, brothers, the gospel that I proclaimed to
you, which you accepted, on which you have taken your stand,*

*² and by which you are also being saved if you hold firmly to the message I
proclaimed to you—unless, of course, your faith was worthless.*

*³ For I passed on to you the most important points of what I received: Christ
died for our sins in keeping with the Scriptures,*

*⁴ he was buried, he was raised on the third day in keeping with the Scrip-
tures—and is still alive!—(ISV).*

Receive Christ. Believe with your heart. Confess with your mouth.

In Romans, we are told how to personally receive Christ: *"That if thou
shalt confess with thy mouth the Lord Jesus, and shalt believe in thine heart that
God hath raised him from the dead, thou shalt be saved. For with the heart man
believeth unto righteousness; and with the mouth confession is made unto salvation" (Romans 10:9, 10 [KJV]).*

Pray this prayer if you want to receive Jesus Christ as your Lord and Savior, and remember that the prayer in itself does not save you, but God to

Whom you are praying does. The prayer verbally communicates to God your heart's desire for Him to forgive you through His Son Jesus Christ as you repent of your sin and begin to trust and obey Him. Confess with your mouth that you have sinned. Turn from your sin and accept Jesus' sacrifice on your behalf. Ask Him into your life. Choose to obey God from now on. He will forgive you and be with you always.

Pray as follows:

Father, I come to You right now, in the Name of Jesus Christ. Lord, I need Your forgiveness because I have sinned against You. I give all my heart, mind, soul, and strength to You now. Thank You, Father, for sending Your Son to die for my sin on the cross and raising Him again on the third day for me. I am Yours, Lord, and You are mine. I truly believe and will trust in You alone for my salvation from this day forward. I surrender my life to You as my Savior and my Lord. I receive You now into my heart and life. Help me, Lord, to please You with my life. In Jesus' Name I pray. Amen.

Congratulations! You are now a follower of Jesus Christ. Get yourself into a healthy and well-balanced church. Get baptized. Study your Bible to learn about Christ daily, and obey God's Word. Pray daily, and fellowship with other believers. Tell people about your decision to follow Christ, and share the hope of the Gospel with others in gentleness, respect, and love. Amen!

Recommended Reading:

The Holy Bible, beginning with the Gospel of John

The Commands of Christ

Jesus Christ told us many commands throughout His earthly ministry. Below are many of them.

The Foundational Commands
1. You must be born again (John 3:5-7).
2. Love God above all else (Matthew 22:37-39).
3. Love your neighbor as yourself (Matthew 27:37-39).
4. Imitate the Good Samaritan in your life (Luke 10:37).
5. Treat others as you want to be treated (Luke 6:21).

God's Terms
6. Repent (Matthew 4:17).
7. Ask, seek, and knock (Matthew 7:7-8).
8. Fear God (Luke 12:5).
9. Believe the Gospel (Mark 1:15).
10. Have faith in God (Mark 11:22).
11. Receive God's power (Luke 24:49).
12. Keep your word (Matthew 5:33-37).
13. Don't put God to the test (Matthew 4:7).
14. Worship and serve God only (Matthew 4:10).
15. Come to Me if you are thirsty (John 7:37).
16. Trust in Jesus as you would trust in God (John 14:1).

17. Come to Me if you are weary (Matthew 11:28).

18. Take My yoke upon you (Matthew 11:29).

19. Come, follow Me (Matthew 4:19; Matthew 16:24).

20. Let the dead bury the dead (Matthew 8:22).

Obeying Jesus Christ

21. Obey My commands (John 14:15, 23-24).

22. Choose the narrow way (Matthew 7:13-14).

23. Strive to enter in through the narrow gate (Matthew 7:13; Luke 13:24).

24. Do not commit adultery (Matthew 5:27-30).

25. Beware of covetousness (Luke 12:15).

26. Hear, if you have ears to hear (Mark 4:19).

27. Be a wise man (Matthew 7:24-27).

28. Walk while you still have the light (John 12:35-36).

29. Cut off anything that causes you to sin (Matthew 8:8-9).

30. Remain in My love (John 15:10).

31. Abide in Me (John 15:9).

32. Be perfect, as God is perfect (Matthew 5:48).

33. Bear your own cross (Luke 14:27).

34. Feed my sheep (John 21:15-16).

35. Watch and pray (Matthew 26:41).

36. Celebrate the Lord's Supper (Matthew 26:26-27).

37. Love your neighbor (Matthew 22:39).

38. Love the Lord (Matthew 22:37).

39. Hear God's voice (Matthew 11:15).

40. Do unto others as you want them to do to you (Matthew 7:12).

41. Do not lust (Matthew 5:28-30).

42. Honor God's law (Matthew 5:17-19).

43. Let your light shine (Matthew 5:16).

44. Keep your word (Matthew 5:37).

Loving, Forgiving, and Judging

45. Care for My sheep (John 21:15-17).

46. Love each other as I have loved you (John 13:34).

47. Don't lord it over one another (Luke 22:25-26).

48. Don't murmur amongst yourselves (John 6:43).

49. Don't condemn others (Luke 6:37).

50. Judge righteously and not by appearance (John 7:24).

51. Have salt amongst yourself and peace with one another (Mark 9:50).

52. Reconcile with your brother before making your offering to God (Matthew 5:23-24).

53. Examine yourself before correcting your brother (Matthew 7:5).

54. If your brother sins against you, talk to him privately and show him his fault (Matthew 18:15).

55. If your brother habitually sins, rebuke him (Luke 17:3).

56. If your brother says, "I repent," forgive him (Luke 17:4).

57. If he who sinned doesn't listen to you, involve two or three witnesses (Matthew 18:16).

58. If he who sinned doesn't listen to the two or three witnesses, involve the whole Church (Matthew 18:17).

59. If he who sinned doesn't listen to the Church, treat him as an unbeliever (Matthew 18:17).

60. Be merciful, as God is merciful (Luke 6:36).

61. Honor your parents (Matthew 15:4).

Prayer and Fasting

62. Fast in secret (Matthew 6:16-18).

63. Pray in secret (Matthew 6:5-6).

64. Be alert and pray, so that you do not fall into temptation (Matthew 26:41).

65. When praying, follow the pattern in "Our Lord's Prayer" (Matthew 6:9-13; Luke 11:2-4).

66. Don't use vain repetition when you pray (Matthew 6:7-8).

67. When praying, forgive others (Mark 11:25).

68. Ask God to send workers to the field (Matthew 9:38).

69. Believe that you will receive what you are asking for in prayer (Mark 11:24).

Religion

70. Make sure that the light you believe you have is not darkness (Luke 11:35).
71. Don't think that I have come to abolish the law or the prophets—but know that I have come to fulfill them (Matthew 5:17).
72. Be careful how you hear (Luke 8:18).
73. Be careful of false prophets (Matthew 7:15).
74. Share bread and wine in remembrance of Me (Luke 22:19).
75. Let your "yes" be "yes" and your "no" be "no" (Matthew 5:37).

Persecution and Enemies

76. Don't fear those who can kill your body (Luke 12:4).
77. Be encouraged during difficult times (John 16:33).
78. Deny yourself, carry your cross, and follow Me (Mark 8:34).
79. Remember that if they hate Me, they will also hate you (Matthew 10:24-25; John 15:20).
80. Don't be troubled or afraid (John 14:27).
81. Don't resist the person who wrongs you (Matthew 5:39).
82. Love your enemies, and do good to those who hate you (Luke 6:27).
83. Rejoice and leap for joy when you are persecuted because of Me (Matthew 5:12; Luke 6:22-23).
84. Pray for those who persecute you (Matthew 5:44).
85. Agree with your adversary quickly (Matthew 5:41).
86. When they persecute you in one city, flee to another (Matthew 10:23).
87. Do more than what you are obligated to do (Matthew 5:41).
88. Turn the other cheek to the one that hurts you (Luke 6:29).
89. Fear not (Matthew 10:28).

Money and Possessions

90. Don't accumulate treasures on earth—but in heaven (Matthew 6:19-20).
91. Give to the poor of what you have (Luke 11:41).
92. Invite those who cannot return the favor (Luke 14:12-13).

93. When you give to the needy, do it in secret (Matthew 6:3-4).
94. Be generous (Luke 6:38).
95. Give to those who ask (Matthew 5:42).
96. To those who ask, don't turn away (Matthew 5:42).
97. If someone takes legal action against you, give more than the person asks (Matthew 5:40).
98. Do good and lend—without expecting anything in return (Luke 6:35).
99. Don't do your righteousness in order to be seen by others (Matthew 6:1-2).
100. If someone takes what is yours, don't try to claim it back (Luke 6:30).
101. Don't turn the house of God into a marketplace (John 2:16).
102. Give to Caesar what is his—and give to God what belongs to God (Matthew 22:21).

Working for God and Living by Faith
103. Don't work for physical food—but spiritual food (John 6:27).
104. You cannot serve both God and mammon (Matthew 6:24).
105. Don't worry about your life—what you will eat, drink, or wear (Matthew 6:25-30).
106. Freely give as you have freely received (Matthew 10:8).
107. Make the Kingdom of God and His righteousness your top priority (Matthew 6:33).
108. Don't worry about the future (Matthew 6:34).

Preaching the Teachings of Jesus
109. Preach the Gospel to everyone (Mark 16:15).
110. Make disciples — baptizing them and teaching them to keep what I have commanded you (Matthew 28:19-20).
111. Open your eyes and see that the harvest is ready — right now (John 4:35).
112. Shine your light by doing good works (Matthew 5:16).
113. Preach repentance and forgiveness of sins in Jesus' name (Luke 24:47).

114. Be wise like a serpent, but innocent like doves (Matthew 10:16).

115. Don't give what is holy to the dogs; don't cast your pearls before the swine (Matthew 7:6).

Marriage and Children

116. What God has joined in marriage, man should not separate (Matthew 19:6).

117. Let the children come to Jesus (Matthew 19:14).

118. Don't despise little ones (Matthew 18:10).

Keeping Watch and the Last Days

119. Stay alert and be prepared (Matthew 24:42-44).

120. Don't believe those that say, "Christ is here," or "Christ is there" (Matthew 24:23-26).

121. Be careful that nobody deceives you (Matthew 24:4-5).

122. Keep watch, and pray, and present yourself worthy unto Christ (Matthew 24:42, 44; Luke 21:36).

123. When you hear of wars and revolutions, don't be afraid (Luke 21:9).

124. When you see the sun darkening, the moon not giving light, and stars falling—know that My coming is near (Matthew 24:29-33).

125. Expect earthquakes, disease, famine, and wars (Matthew 24:7).

126. Await My return (Matthew 24:42-44).

Humility and Discipline

127. Clean yourself internally, in your spirit (Matthew 23:26).

128. Don't sit in a place of honor, but take the lowest seat (Luke 14:8-10).

129. Don't rejoice over having spiritual power, but that you have eternal life (Luke 10:20).

After we have completed all these things that Jesus has commanded, we must remember that we have only accomplished what is our duty (Luke 17:10).

Conclusion

When I came to the saving knowledge of Jesus Christ, my goals and motives in this life were changed for both time and eternity. I now live with a desire to please God with my life in the things I say, do, and think.

I hope this book helps you better understand what it means to be *In Christ's Service.* One of my main goals for writing this book is to help the Body of Christ understand God's Truth better as He has revealed it in His Word. I desire that everyone be a disciple *In Christ's Service,* rightly dividing the Word of Truth (**2 Ti. 2:15**), worshiping God in Spirit and Truth (**Jn. 4:24**), ready to give an answer to anyone who asks about the hope that is in us with gentleness and respect (**1 Pe. 3:15**), loving God with all our heart, mind, soul, and strength (**Mk. 12:30**).

Thank you for taking the time to read this book. To God be all the glory all the time!

In Christ's service,
David Wayne Meeker

In Christ's Service

Study Guide

How to Use This Study Guide

This study guide features nine categories in twelve study lessons and can be adapted to a 21-week curriculum by combining the individual sessions at two hours per study, per week as follows:

Weeks One & Two: Study 1	Week Eleven: Study 7
Weeks Three & Four: Study 2	Weeks Twelve & Thirteen: Study 8
Weeks Five & Six: Study 3	Weeks Fourteen & Fifteen: Study 9
Weeks Seven & Eight: Study 4	Weeks Sixteen & Seventeen: Study 10
Week Nine: Study 5	Weeks Eighteen & Nineteen: Study 11
Week Ten: Study 6	Weeks Twenty & Twenty-One: Study 12

To help facilitate both study guide leaders and students, the lessons are arranged as follows:

- The Bible
- Obedience
- Prayer

- Worship and Praise
- Fellowship
- Evangelism
- Discipleship
- Baptism
- Salvation

The content of the study guide is concise and is designed to build up and equip the body of Christ. Understanding God's Word is foundationally important in knowing God, as we reach the lost with the Gospel of Jesus Christ in this generation.

1

The Bible, Part 1

A. Why should we study the Bible? (See Ps. 119:9, 11, 162; Ro. 10:17; 15:4; 2 Th. 2:15; 2 Ti. 2:15; 3:16, 17; Ja. 1:22.)

B. Who wrote the Bible? (See 2 Ti. 3:16; 2 Pe. 1:20, 21.)

C. Can the Bible be understood by the unbeliever? (See 1 Co. 2:13-16.)

D. How should we respond to the Bible? (See Jb. 23:12; Jn. 6:68; 1 Jn. 2:5; 2 Ti. 4:2; Jude 1:3.)

E. What are some of the benefits from studying the Bible? (See Ps. 119:105; Lu. 11:28; Jn. 17:17; Ep. 6:13-17.)

F. What does the Bible say is sin? (See Ex. 20:1-17; 1 Sa. 15:23; Ps. 51:5; Ro. 3:23; 6:23; 1 Ti. 6:9; Ja. 1:14, 15; 1 Jn. 3:4.)

2

The Bible, Part 2

G. What does the Bible say about Jesus Christ? (See Ps. 118:22; Is. 9:6; 53:3-12; Lu. 1:26-35; Jn. 1:1-5; 4:25, 26; 5:22; Ac. 3:15; Ro. 1:3, 4; 6:11; 10:9, 10; 2 Co. 5:17, 19; Col. 1:18, 19; 2:9, 10; 1 Ti. 6:15; Tit. 2:13, 14; 1 Jn. 1:1; Re. 1:18.)

H. What does the Bible say about the Holy Spirit? (See Ge. 1:1, 2; Ps. 51:11; 139:7, 8; Mt. 12:28, 31, 32; 28:19; Lu. 4:14; Jn. 14:16-18, 26; 15:26; 16:7-14; Ac. 1:8; 5:3, 4; 10:19, 21; Ro. 8:2-11, 26, 27; 15:16; 1 Co. 2:10; 12:7-11; Ga. 5:22, 23; Ep. 4:30; Tit. 3:5, 6.)

I. What does the Bible say about God? (See Ge. 1:1; De. 7:9; Ne. 9:31; Ps. 34:8; 46:1; 50:1; 62:6; 71:5; 75:1; Is. 25:8; 42:8; Mt. 3:16, 17; 6:9; Lu. 1:37; Ro. 1:20; 11:33; Ep. 1:17; 2:8-10; 1 Th. 1:9; He. 11:6; 1 Jn. 4:8, 16; Ja. 4:8, 12; Re. 1:8.)

J. What does the Bible say about God's will? (See Ex. 20:1; Pr. 16:3; Am. 5:24; Mk. 10:45; Jn. 3:16; 6:40; 1 Co. 14:1; 1 Th. 4:3-5.)

K. What does the Bible say about the Bible? (See Ps. 18:30; 33:4; 119:89, 99, 100, 138; Jn. 17:17; Ac. 18:28; Ro. 1:1, 2; 1 Co. 2:12-16; Ga. 3:10; Ep. 6:17; 2 Ti. 3:16; He. 4:12; 1 Pe. 2:2.)

L. What does the Bible say about satan? (See Jb. 1:6-12; Mt. 4:1-11; Jn. 8:44; Ep. 6:12; 1 Ti. 4:1; 1Pe. 5:8; Ja. 4:7; 1 Jn. 3:7, 8; Re. 20:10.)

M. Does the Bible reveal the Trinity? (See Ge. 1:26; 3:22; Mt. 28:19; Lu. 3:22; Jn. 14:26; 1 Jn. 5:7.)

3

Obedience

A. What does the Bible say about obedience, and is it important? (See 2 Ki. 18:6; Ps. 119:30, 60; 143:10; Pr. 3:1, 2; Ec. 12:13; Lu. 6:46-49; Jn. 14:15, 21, 24; Jn. 15:10; Ac. 5:29; Ro. 6:16; Ph. 2:12; 1 Pe. 1:2; 1 Jn. 2:3; 3:24; 5:3; Ja. 1:22-25.)

B. What are the blessings of obedience? (See Jsh. 1:8; 1 Sa. 15:22; Is. 1:19; Lu. 11:28; Jn. 8:51; 2 Co. 5:17; Ep. 6:5-9; He. 5:9; Ja. 1:21; 1 Pe. 1:22.)

C. What are the curses of disobedience? (See Mt. 7:21; 25:46; Lu. 6:46; Jn. 3:36; Ro. 6:23; Col. 3:5, 6; 2 Th. 1:8; Re. 20:12.)

4

Prayer

A. What does the Bible say about prayer? (See Je. 33:3; Mk. 11:24; Lu. 22:40; Jn. 15:7; 2 Co. 13:7, 9; Ep. 6:18, 19; Ph. 4:6; 1 Th. 5:17, 25; Ja. 5:13-16.)

B. In Whose Name should we pray? (See Ep. 5:20; Col. 3:17; 2 Th. 3:6.)

C. To Whom should we pray? (See Lu. 11:2; Jn. 16:23-26, 17:1, 11, 24, 25.)

D. Does God answer all prayers? (See Jn. 9:31; 15:7; Ja. 4:3.)

E. Where and when should we pray? (See Lu. 6:12; 18:1; Ac. 12:5; Ep. 6:18, 19; 1 Th. 5:17; 2 Th. 1:11; 3:1, 2; 1 Ti. 2:8.)

F. How should we pray? (See Mt. 6:6, 9-13; Lu. 11:1-4; 18:9-14; Ja. 1:1-8; 4:3; 1 Jn. 5:14.)

G. Are there hindrances to prayer? (See Jn. 9:31; 1 Pe. 3:7.)

5

Worship & Praise

A. What does the Bible say about worship and praise? (See Ex. 33:10; 34:14; Ps. 7:17; 8:1; 9:1, 2; 29:1, 2; 63:3, 4; 100:4; Mt. 2:2; Lu. 4:8; 1 Th. 5:16-18; He. 12:28.)

B. Why should we worship and praise? (See Ps. 21:13; 22:23; 29:2; 95:1-6; Is. 12:5; Ac. 17:24; He. 12:28; Re. 4:11.)

C. How should we worship and praise? (See Ps. 71:8; 95:6; Jn. 4:23, 24; Ro. 12:1, 2; Col. 3:13-17; He. 12:28.)

6

Fellowship

A. What does the Bible say about fellowship and is it important? (See Jn. 17:21; Ac. 2:42, 44; Ga. 6:2, 10; Col. 2:2; 3:16; 1 Th. 5:11; He. 10:25; Ja. 5:16; 1 Pe. 3:8.)

B. With whom should Christians have fellowship? (See Mt. 12:48-50; 2 Co. 6:14-18; Ep. 5:11; 1 Jn. 1:3-7.)

C. Should there be unity in our fellowship? (See 1 Co. 1:10; 2 Co. 6:14-18; Ep. 5:19; 2 Th. 3:6.)

D. How should our conduct be in fellowship? (See Ep. 4:1-3; Ph. 2:2-5.)

7

Evangelism

A. What does the Bible say about evangelism and is it important? (See Is. 43:10; Mt. 5:14-16; 28:18-20; Ro. 10:15; 1 Co. 1:23, 24; 2 Co. 5:20; 2 Ti. 4:2; 1 Pe. 3:15.)

B. Who should evangelize? (See Mt. 5:14-16; 28:18-20.)

C. Whose work is salvation and Who gives us power to evangelize? (See Jn. 3:6, 7; Ac. 1:8.)

D. Why should we evangelize? (See Lu. 24:46, 47; Ro. 10:13-17.)

E. Should we be bold in our evangelism? (See Mt. 10:33; Ep. 6:19.)

F. What does the Bible say about the conduct of the Gospel? (See Mt. 4:23; 10:33; Mk. 16:15; Jude 1:3; Ro. 1:16; 1 Co. 9:16; Ga. 1:6-8; Ph. 1:27; 1 Th. 1:5; 2 Ti. 1:8.)

G. Was evangelism important to Jesus? (See Mt. 9:37; 28:18-20; Mk. 16:15; Lu. 10:1, 2.)

8

Discipleship

A. What does the Bible say about discipleship? (See Mt. 28:19, 20; 16:24, 25; Lu. 6:40; 14:33; Jn. 15:1-17.)

B. Was discipleship important to Jesus? (See Mt. 28:18-20.)

C. Who are disciples? (See Mt. 16:24; Mk. 8:34; Jn. 8:31; 2 Ti. 2:15.)

D. What are some of the things a disciple must do? (See Mt. 5:14, 15; 28:19, 20; Lu. 14:27, 33; Jn. 8:31, 32; 13:35; 15:12; 2 Co. 5:20; Ep. 4:12; 5:19, 21; 2 Ti. 2:2; Tit. 2:1.)

E. Should we disciple others? (See Mt. 28:18-20; Ac. 14:21, 22.)

F. How do we identify disciples? (See Mt. 13:23; Lu. 8:15; Jn. 3:3; Ro. 8:9; 2 Co. 5:17-20; Ga. 5:22-24; Ep. 5:1, 2; 1 Jn. 2:5; 3:9.)

9

Baptism

A. What does water baptism symbolize? (See Ro. 6:1-6; Col. 2:12.)

B. When should water baptism be done? (See Mt. 28:18-20; Ac. 2:38.)

C. Is water baptism necessary for salvation? (See Lu. 7:50; 23:39-43; Ac. 10:44-48.)

D. For whom is water baptism? (See Ac. 8:13, 36-38; Ro. 6:1-6.)

E. Did Christ send Paul to baptize? (See 1 Co. 1:17.)

F. Did Christ baptize anyone? (See Jn. 4:1, 2.)

10

Salvation

A. What does the Bible say about the Gospel? (See Mt. 28:18-20; Lu. 24:46, 47; Jn. 1:12; 3:36; 5:24; 6:40; Ro. 1:16; 1 Co. 15:1-8; 1 Th. 1:4, 5.)

B. What does the Bible say about eternal life? (See Mt. 7:21; Jn. 3:15-18; 3:36; 5:24; 6:40, 47, 68; 17:3; Ro. 6:23; 10:13-17; Ep. 2:8, 9; Tit. 3:7.)

C. What does the Bible say about the atonement? (See Le. 17:11; 1 Co. 15:3; Tit. 2:13, 14; 1 Pe. 3:18.)

D. Is repentance necessary for salvation? (See Lu. 13:3-5; 15:7; Ac. 17:30; 2 Pe. 3:9; 1 Jn. 1:9.)

11

E. What is God's plan of salvation? (See Jn. 3:16-18.)

F. Why should we receive Christ? (See Jn. 14:16; Ac. 16:30, 31; Ro. 3:23, 24; 1 Jn. 5:10-13.)

G. What does the Bible say about the cross? (See Ep. 2:16; Col. 1:20-22; 2:11-16.)

H. Can we earn salvation through our own effort apart from Christ? (See Jn. 3:16-18; Ro. 6:23; Ep. 2:8, 9; 1 Ti. 2:5.)

I. Is Jesus the only way to eternal life? (See Jn. 3:36; 14:6; Ac. 4:12; Ro. 6:23; 1 Jn. 1:8, 9; 4:15.)

J. What does the Bible say about grace through Christ? (See Ep. 2:1-10.)

12

K. What does the Bible say about the Book of Life? (See Ph. 4:3; Re. 3:5; 20:15; 21:27.)

L. What does the Bible say about Heaven? (See Ge. 14:22; Is. 65:17; Mt. 5:17-20; 7:13, 14; Jn. 14:2, 3; 2 Co. 5:1; Ph. 1:23; 3:21; Ja. 1:17; 2 Pe. 3:13; Re. 5:9-13; 7:17; 21:3, 4; 22:5.)

M. Who will go to Heaven? (See Mt. 5:3; 19:14; Jn. 3:16; 14:6; Ro. 10:9; 1 Jn. 4:17.)

N. What does the Bible say about hell? (See Mt. 5:29, 30; 7:13; 8:12; 10:28; 13:49, 50; 25:41, 46; Lu. 16:22-24; 2 Th. 1:8; 2 Pe. 2:4-9; Jude 1:7; Re. 19:20; 20:10; 21:8.)

O. Who will be sent to hell? (See Jude 1:15; Re. 20:15.)

Examine Yourself Test

Keep examining yourself to see whether you are continuing in the faith. Test yourself! Test yourself to see if Jesus Christ lives in you. Examine yourself to make certain you are not failing the test! —2 Corinthians 13:5 (ISV).

1. Do you believe in Jesus Christ?
Yes☐   No☐   Seldom☐

1 John 5:13 I have written these things to you who believe in the name of the Son of God so that you may know that you have eternal life (ISV).

1 John 5:1 Everyone who believes that Jesus is the Christ has been born from God, and everyone who loves the parent also loves the child (ISV).

2. Do you practice sin regularly?
Yes☐   No☐   Seldom☐

1 John 3:9 No one who has been born from God practices sin, because God's seed abides in him.

Indeed, he cannot go on sinning, because he has been born from God (ISV).

Romans 6:1 What should we say, then? Should we go on sinning so that grace may increase?

Romans 6:2 Of course not! How can we who died as far as sin is concerned go on living in it? (ISV).

3. Do you study God's Word daily?
   Yes☐   No☐   Seldom☐

2 Timothy 2:15 Do your best to present yourself to God as an approved worker who has nothing to be ashamed of, handling the word of truth with precision (ISV).

2 Timothy 3:16 All Scripture is God-breathed and is useful for teaching, for reproof, for correction, and for training in righteousness, (ISV).

4. Do you abide in Christ?
   Yes☐   No☐   Seldom☐

John 15:4 Abide in me, and I in you. As the branch cannot bear fruit by itself, unless it abides in the vine, neither can you, unless you abide in me (ISV).

John 15:5 I am the vine; you are the branches. Whoever abides in me and I in him, he it is that bears much fruit, for apart from me you can do nothing (ISV).

5. Are you indifferent to sin?
   Yes☐   No☐   Seldom☐

1 John 1:6 If we say that we have fellowship with Him and walk in darkness, we lie and do not practice the truth.

1 John 1:7 But if we walk in the light, as He is in the light, we have fellowship with one another, and the blood of Jesus Christ His Son cleanses us from all sin.

1 John 1:8 If we say that we have no sin, we deceive ourselves, and the truth is not in us (ESV).

6. Do you obey Christ?
   Yes☐   No☐   Seldom☐

1 John 2:3 And by this we know that we have known Him, if we keep His commandments.

1 John 2:4 He who says, I have known Him, and does not keep His commandments, is a liar, and the truth is not in him.

1 John 2:5 But whoever keeps His Word, truly in this one the love of God is perfected. By this we know that we are in Him.

1 John 2:6 He who says he abides in Him ought himself also to walk even as He walked (ESV).

7. Do you practice righteousness?
Yes☐   No☐   Seldom☐

1 John 3:7 Little children, let no one deceive you. He who does righteousness is righteous, even as that One is righteous (KJV).

8. Do you pray for the lost?
Yes☐   No☐   Seldom☐

Matthew 9:37 Then he said to his disciples, "The harvest is plentiful, but the laborers are few;

Matthew 9:38 therefore pray earnestly to the Lord of the harvest to send out laborers into his harvest" (ESV).

9. Do you go to church regularly?
Yes☐   No☐   Seldom☐

Hebrews 10:25 not forsaking the assembling of ourselves together, as the manner of some is, but exhorting one another, and so much the more as you see the Day approaching (ISV).

10. Do you pray to God daily?
Yes☐   No☐   Seldom☐

1 Thessalonians 5:17 pray without ceasing,

1 Thessalonians 5:18 give thanks in all circumstances; for this is the will of God in Christ Jesus for you (ESV).

1 Timothy 2:8 I desire then that in every place the men should pray, lifting holy hands without anger or quarreling; (ESV).

11. Do you share the Gospel regularly?
Yes☐   No☐   Seldom☐

2 Timothy 1:8 Therefore do not be ashamed of the testimony about our Lord, nor of me his prisoner, but share in suffering for the gospel by the power of God,

2 Timothy 1:9 who saved us and called us to a holy calling, not because of our works but because of his own purpose and grace, which he gave us in Christ Jesus before the ages began, (ESV).

12. Do you keep yourself pure?
Yes☐   No☐   Seldom☐

1 John 5:18 We know that the person who has been born from God does not go on sinning. Rather, the Son of God protects them, and the evil one cannot harm them (ISV).

13. Do you love your neighbor?
Yes☐   No☐   Seldom☐

Matthew 22:37 And he said to him, "You shall love the Lord your God with all your heart and with all your soul and with all your mind.

Matthew 22:38 This is the great and first commandment.

Matthew 22:39 And a second is like it: You shall love your neighbor as yourself (ESV).

14. Do you believe that Jesus is God?
Yes☐   No☐   Seldom☐

John 1:1 In the beginning was the Word, and the Word was with God, and the Word was God (KJV).

Colossians 2:9 For in Him dwells all the fullness of the Godhead bodily (KJV).

15. Do you know and love Christ?
Yes☐   **No**☐   **Seldom**☐

John 14:15 If you love Me, keep My commandments (ISV).

1 John 2:3 This is how we can be sure that we have come to know him: if we continually keep his commandments.

1 John 2:4 The person who says, "I have come to know him," but does not continually keep his commandments is a liar, and the truth is not in that person.

1 John 2:5 But whoever continually keeps his word is the kind of person in whom God's love has truly been perfected. This is how we can be sure that we are in union with him: (ISV).

16. Do you worship God daily?
Yes☐   **No**☐   **Seldom**☐

Psalm 59:16 But I will sing of thy strength; Yea, I will sing aloud of thy lovingkindness in the morning: For thou hast been my high tower, And a refuge in the day of my distress (KJV).

Psalm 63:3 Because thy lovingkindness is better than life, My lips shall praise thee.

Psalm 63:4 So will I bless thee while I live: I will lift up my hands in thy name (KJV).

17. Do you desire to serve others?
Yes☐   **No**☐   **Seldom**☐

Galatians 5:13 For you, brothers, were called to freedom. Only do not turn your freedom into an opportunity to gratify your flesh, but through love make it your habit to serve one another (ISV).

Ephesians 6:7 Serve willingly, as if you were serving the Lord and not merely people (ISV).

18. Do you love the things of this world?

Yes☐ No☐ Seldom☐

Titus 2:12 training us to renounce ungodliness and worldly passions, and to live self-controlled, upright, and godly lives in the present age, (ESV).

1 John 5:4 because everyone who is born from God has overcome the world. Our faith is the victory that overcomes the world.

1 John 5:5 Who overcomes the world? Is it not the person who believes that Jesus is the Son of God? (ISV).

19. Do you love other Christians?

Yes☐ No☐ Seldom☐

1 John 3:14 We know that we have passed out of death into life, because we love the brothers. Whoever does not love abides in death (ESV).

John 13:34 "I am giving you a new commandment to love one another. Just as I have loved you, you also should love one another.

John 13:35 This is how everyone will know that you are my disciples, if you have love for one another" (ISV).

20. Do you forgive others?

Yes☐ No☐ Seldom☐

Mark 11:26 But if you do not forgive, neither will your Father in Heaven forgive your trespasses (ESV).

21. Do you enjoy reading your Bible?

Yes☐ No☐ Seldom☐

2 Timothy 3:16 All Scripture is God-breathed and is useful for teaching, for reproof, for correction, and for training in righteousness,

2 Timothy 3:17 so that the man of God may be complete and thoroughly equipped for every good work (ISV).

22. Do you love God with all your heart, mind, soul, and strength?
Yes□ No□ Seldom□

Mark 12:30 'and you must love the Lord your God with all your heart, with all your soul, with all your mind, and with all your strength' (ISV).

23. Do you desire to serve the Lord?
Yes□ No□ Seldom□

Romans 12:11 Never be lazy in showing such devotion. Be on fire with the Spirit. Serve the Lord (ISV).

24. Do you confess your sin?
Yes□ No□ Seldom□

1 John 1:9 If we confess our sins, he is faithful and just to forgive us our sins and to cleanse us from all unrighteousness (ESV).

Romans 6:1 What shall we say then? Are we to continue in sin that grace may abound?

Romans 6:2 By no means! How can we who died to sin still live in it? (ESV)

25. Is your life dedicated to Jesus?
Yes□ No□ Seldom□

Matthew 10:33 but whoever denies me before men, I also will deny before my Father who is in heaven (ESV).

Matthew 16:24 Then Jesus told his disciples, "If anyone would come after me, let him deny himself and take up his cross and follow me" (ESV).

26. Do you believe that Christ is the only way to Heaven?
Yes□ No□ Seldom□

John 14:6 Jesus said to him, "I am the way, and the truth, and the life. No one comes to the Father except through me. (ESV)

1 Timothy 2:5 For there is one God, and there is one mediator between God and men, the man Christ Jesus, (ESV)

Terms and Definitions

Adoption The giving to anyone the same name and privileges of a child who is not a child by birth. This term is found in the New Testament in Paul's letters. It is the process by which a man or woman might be brought into God's family, with all the same benefits and privileges through Jesus Christ (Jn. 1:12; Ro. 8:15, 23; Ga. 3:26; 4:5; Ep. 1:5).

Apologetics The English word comes from a Greek root meaning "to defend, to make reply, to give an answer, to legally defend oneself." In the New Testament times apologia was a formal courtroom defense of something (2 Ti. 4:16).

Apostle A title referencing any of Jesus' 12 disciples after the resurrection of Christ, but sometimes referencing other Christ-followers with whom Jesus revealed Himself physically after the resurrection, such as Paul (Ac. 9:1-19; 22:6-21; 26:12-18).

Atonement The repair of the broken relationship between God and man restored by the death and resurrection of Jesus Christ (Ex. 12:5; Le. 17:11; Is. 53:3-12; Lu. 4:18, 19; Jn. 3:16; 10:17; Ac. 20:28; Ro. 3:23-25; 1 Co. 7:23; 15:3; Ep. 2:13; Col. 1:12, 13; Tit. 2:14; He. 9:22; 1 Pe. 2:21-24; 3:18).

Belief The thing believed. Our belief is only as true, reliable, and good as the object in which it is placed. Christ is the object in which Christian belief is placed. Our Christian belief is in the person of Jesus Christ (Mk. 1:15; Ac. 20:21; Ro. 10:9; 2 Th. 2:13).

Body of Christ Christians make up the Body of Christ (1 Co. 12:27). Jesus is the head of the body (Col. 1:18) and should be the center of everything we say, do, and think (Mt.18:20). The Body of Christ meets together to pray (Ep. 6:18), worship (Ex. 34:14), share in suffering (2 Ti. 2:3), encourage (Ep. 4:12), and teach (2 Ti. 2:2) about Christ in love (Jn. 13:34) and unity (Ep. 4:3). The Body of Christ is responsible for the preaching of the Gospel to others (Mt. 28:18, 19) with gentleness and respect (1 Pe. 3:15).

Conversion The moment an individual repents and places his or her faith upon Jesus for his or her salvation. When the individual is declared righteous and forgiven by God, thus converted from being far from God to now being accepted and justified in Christ (2 Chr. 7:14; Jn.3:5; Ac. 2:38; Ro.12:2; 2 Co. 5:17; Ep. 4:22; Re. 3:20).

Covenant A treaty, or promise, between two people or groups. Biblically, it is a promise made by God to His people for salvation (Je. 31:31-34; Mt. 26:28; Lu. 22:20; He. 8:6, 8; 9:15; 12:24; 13:20; 1 Co. 11:25).

Cult A cult is a religious group that denies one or more of the fundamentals of Biblical truth. Specifically, it is a group that claims to be Christian but whose teachings, if believed, would prevent someone from having a saving relationship with Jesus Christ (Col. 2:8; 1 Ti. 6:20).

Disciple A person who follows a teacher. This person does what his or her teacher says to do (Lu. 11:28; Jn. 14:15; 1 Ti. 6:14; Ja. 1:22; 1 Jn. 5:3).

Doctrine, Biblical A statement(s) describing a set of beliefs that is grounded in the Word of God and theologically sound.

Doubt A lack of faith or trust in something or someone. To not be sure (Pr. 3:5-8; Mt. 21:21; Mk. 11:22-25; He. 11:6; Ja. 1:5-8).

Doxology The study or act of worship by which believers ascribe worth, glory, and praise to God.

Election In the New Testament it occurs six times (Ro. 9:11; 11:5, 7, 28; 1 Th. 1:4; 2 Pe. 1:10). In all these passages it appears to denote an act of Divine selection upon human beings to bring them into a special and saving relationship with God.

Evil Bad. Wicked. Doing things that do not please God (Pr. 8:13; Is. 5:20; Ro. 3:23; 12:9; Ep. 6:12; 1 Th. 5:22).

Expiation Since the prefix *ex* means "out of" or "from," *expiation* has to do with removing something or taking something away. In Biblical terms, it has to do with taking away guilt through the payment of a penalty or offering of atonement.

Fact An isolated piece of information that is indisputable. Information used as evidence or as part of a news report, news article, or evidence in a legal court case.

Faith The on-going and personal commitment to trust and believe. What we believe. We can only be a Christian if we have faith in Christ (Ga. 3:26; Ep. 3:7). Our faith is the relationship we have with God through Jesus Christ (Jn. 14:6). Faith justifies not on its own worthiness and value, but by the worthiness and value of Him in Whom is our faith (Ac. 20:21; Col. 2:9). Faith makes the connection, by which our sin is imputed to Christ, and Christ's righteousness is imputed to us (1 Co. 1:30; 2 Co. 5:19, 21). Without faith, we cannot please God (He. 11:6). We are saved by grace through faith in Christ (Ep. 2:8, 9).

Father, The God. The first person of the Trinity. The Father shares the same attributes and characteristics as Jesus and the Holy Spirit. He is holy (Le. 19:2; Is. 6:3), eternal (De. 33:27; Ps. 90:2), omnipresent (Ps. 139:7-12), omnipotent (Re. 19:6), omniscient (Ps. 139:2-6; Pr. 15:3), immutable (Mal. 3:6), righteous (Ps. 119:137), truth (Je. 10:10), good (Ps. 107:8), merciful (Ps. 103:8-17), gracious (Ps. 111:4), faithful (De. 7:9), and loves us (Jn. 3:16; 1 Jn. 4:8).

Forgiveness An act of pardon by God through the completed work of His Son Jesus Christ. It is a gift from God (Jn. 3:16; Ro. 6:23), through faith (Ro. 10:9, 10, 13; Ep. 2:8, 9) in Jesus Christ (Jn. 10:17). Forgiveness is promised by God when we repent of our sin and believe and trust in Jesus for our salvation (Jn. 3:16-18; 1 Jn. 1:8-10), but we have to forgive others if we want God to forgive us (Ep. 4:32).

God The Creator (Ge. 1:1) of the universe and everything that exists (Ac. 17:24). The Bible teaches that there is one God (1 Ti. 2:5) revealed in three persons — the Father, the Son, and the Holy Spirit (Mt. 3:16, 17; 1 Pe. 1:2) — Who all share the same attributes and characteristics. He is omnipresent (Ps. 139:7-12), omniscient (Ps. 139:2-6; Pr. 15:3), omnipotent (Re. 19:6), eternal (Ps. 45:6), holy (Is. 6:3), righteous (Ps. 119:137), merciful (Ps. 103:8-17), gracious (Ps. 111:4), faithful (De. 7:9), immutable (Mal. 3:6), truthful (Je. 10:10), spirit (Jn. 4:24), good (Ps. 107:8), and love (1 Jn. 4:8).

Gospel, The Paul tells us what the Gospel is — that Christ died for our sin and was buried and rose again on the third day (1 Co. 15:3, 4) to save us from the eternal consequences of our sin (Jn. 3:16). Salvation is a gift from God through faith in Jesus Christ (Ro. 6:23) because He loves us. The Gospel is the grace of God (Jn. 3:16-18; Ac. 13:47; 16:17; 20:24; Ro. 1:16; 1 Co. 1:30; 15:2-6; Ep. 1:7.)

Grace The loving act of God in a person's life, making possible his or her salvation, sanctification, and justification. It is by grace that God makes salvation possible through His Son Jesus Christ's death and resurrection (Ro. 6:23), and it is through grace that He sustains the Body of Christ (Ex. 34:6; Ep. 1:7, 8; 2:8, 9; 1 Pe. 1:13). Grace is a gift from God (Ro. 3:24). God's grace is revealed in His Gospel (Ac. 20:24).

Heaven The dwelling place of God and the hope and destiny of believers of Jesus Christ either by way of the grave or His coming (Is. 25:8; Mt. 5:17-20; 7:13, 14; Jn. 14:2, 3; 2 Co. 5:2; Ph. 1:23; 3:7; Col. 1:5; He. 8:1; 2 Pe. 3:13; Re. 7:17; 21:4; 22:5).

Hell A permanent place of torment for those who are condemned by sin because of their rejection of God's only provision for our sin, His Son Jesus Christ, where they are eternally separated from God in a place of torment (Mt. 8:12; 25:41; Ro. 1:18-20; 2 Pe. 2:4-9; Jude 1:7; Re. 21:8).

Hermeneutics The word *hermeneutics* comes from a Greek root meaning *"Interpreter"* or *"Interpret."* Thus, hermeneutics is an interpretation. *Merriam-Webster Dictionary* defines hermeneutics as *"the study of methodological principles of interpretation (as of the Bible)"* and *"a method or principle of interpretation."* It is also referred to as the *Art and Science of Biblical Interpretation.*

The Holy Bible commands the followers of Christ in 2 Timothy 2:15 to be involved in hermeneutics. The five basic foundational rules of hermeneutics are as follows: **A.**) Scripture must be used to interpret itself. **B.**) Scripture itself is its best commentary. **C.**) Scripture must be taken literally allowing for normal use of figurative language, allegory, narrative, poetry, and parables. **D.**) Scripture must be interpreted in the context by which the passage was originally intended. Correct context will help with determining the correct meaning. **E.**) Be sensitive to the type of literature you are reading. Biblical hermeneutics must also follow these 15 fundamental rules:

1. Understand the author. (Who wrote the book?)
2. Understand the audience. (Why was the book written?)
3. Understand the meaning of words. (*Strong's Dictionary* or *Bible-Works8* is recommended).
4. Understand the historical setting.
5. Understand the grammar.
6. Understand the textual issues.
7. Understand the syntax (the set of rules for the analysis or arrangement of words and phrases to create well-formed sentences in a language).
8. Understand the form and genre of the literature. (Is it legal, historical narrative, figures of speech, analogies, parables, Hebrew poetry and song, wisdom sayings and proverbs, the Gospels, prophecy, genealogy, letters or Epistles, Apocalyptic, etc.?)
9. Understand the immediate context (and remember a text out of context becomes a pretext).
10. Understand the document's context.
11. Understand the author's context.
12. Understand the Biblical context. (Biblical passages are consistent with the whole of Scripture. Scripture is never contradictory of itself).
13. Understand the difference between prescriptive and descriptive statements in the Holy Bible. (Is the verse telling us to do something, or does it describe an action someone does?)

14. Build all doctrine on necessary rather than possible inferences. A necessary inference is something that is clearly taught in Scripture and is conclusive.

15. Interpret the unclear passages in Scripture in light of the clear.

God has given us His Holy Spirit to illuminate His Word and has created us with the ability to logically reason, which includes investigating, analyzing, and reviewing. To understand God's Word correctly is obviously one of the main reasons why God has equipped humans with the capacity for clear and sound reasoning in conducting or assessing factually based information according to strict principles of validity. Biblical interpretation implements the same rules found in the logical reasoning process. He has also given us many people throughout history to help us interpret His Word — which include gifted and anointed Bible teachers (Ep. 4:8-12).

Hypothesis A proposition not yet tested to the point of general acceptance. An un-scientifically supported theory.

Holy Spirit, The God. The third person of the Trinity active in creation (Ge. 1:2; Job 33:4; Ps. 104:30) and throughout history, indwelling believers (Ro. 8:11) and directing and guiding the Church (Jn. 16:12, 13) and is the Source of Scripture. The Holy Spirit shares the same attributes and characteristics in Scripture as the Father and Jesus Christ. He is omnipresent (Ps. 139:7-10), omniscient (Jn. 14:26; 16:12, 13), omnipotent (Lu. 1:35), eternal (He. 9:14), holy (Ro. 1:4), merciful (Ga. 5:22), immutable (Ga. 4:6), truthful (Jn. 16:13), and He teaches (Jn. 14:26), leads us (Ro. 8:14), gives us joy (1 Th. 1:6), seals us (Ep. 4:30), intercedes for us (Ro. 8:26), regenerates us (He. 9:14), reminds us (Jn. 14:26), reveals to us (1 Co. 2:10), communes with us (2 Co. 13:14; 1 Jn. 3:24), convicts us (Jn. 16:8-11) loves us (Ro. 5:5; 15:30; Ga. 5:22), is involved in salvation (Tit. 3:5), and sanctifies us (Ro. 15:16). The Holy Spirit's ministry is both personal and permanent (Jn. 14:16-17).

Imago Dei The Latin translation of "image of God," this term is used to describe God creating mankind in His image and likeness (Ge. 1:26-28), resulting in every single person having immense worth, value, and the unique ability to reflect and connect with God the Creator.

Image of God When the Bible uses the terminology, "created in the image of God" (Ge. 1:26-28), it is talking about the fact that people are made in God's image comprised of mind, emotion, and will. We are able to perceive and feel things and have conscience knowledge of our own abilities and character, having self-awareness. We are moral beings with an inborn 'moral compass," which was given to us from God, as a natural orientation of 'right' and 'wrong.' We have instinctive capacity to develop and appreciate beauty, drama, art, and story in all forms; and we will naturally seek out and develop relationships and friendships with others. We are all this because God is all this, and we are made in God's image and likeness. All these conclusions are consistent with what we observe about ourselves in reality and the overall teachings of the Holy Bible.

Jesus Christ. God The second person of the Trinity. The Creator of the universe and everything that exists (Jn. 1:1-3; Col. 1:16, 17). He is sinless (2 Co. 5:21; 1 Jn. 3:5). Jesus shares the same attributes and characteristics in Scripture as the Father and Holy Spirit. He is omnipresent (Mt. 18:20; 28:18-20), omniscient (Jn. 16:30; 21:17), omnipotent (He. 1:3), eternal (Jn. 1:1, 2; 17:5, 24), holy (Lu. 1:35), righteous (1 Jn. 2:1), merciful (Jude 1:21), faithful (Re. 1:5), immutable (He. 13:8), truthful (Jn. 14:6), good (Lu. 18:18, 19), gracious (1 Pe. 2:3), and loves us (Jn. 15:13; Ga. 2:20). Jesus is called God in the New Testament (Jn. 1:1; 10:20-33; 20:28; Ro. 9:5; Col. 2:9; Tit. 2:13; He. 1:8).

Judgment God will bring every work and secret thing into judgment, whether good or evil, believer or non-believer (Job 34:23; Da. 7:10; Ps. 9:7; Ec. 3:17; 11:9; 12:14; Mal. 3:5; Mt. 12:36; 25:32; Jn. 5:24; 7:24; Ro. 14:10; 1 Co. 3:12-15; 2 Co. 5:10; 2 Ti. 4:8; He. 9:27; 12:23; Re. 11:18; 20:11-15).

Justification The gift of God by which He restores us to a right relationship with Himself through the death and resurrection of His Son Jesus Christ (Ro. 3:23, 24; 1 Jn. 1:9; 2:23, 24; 5:1).

Law, Scientific A statement describing how some phenomena of nature behave. Laws are generalizations from data. They express regularities and patterns in the data. A law is usually limited in scope, to describe a particular process in nature.

Mediator Jesus Christ stands between God and men in establishing our relationship with God. Jesus is the guarantee of our relationship with God. Jesus Christ is the only mediator between God and men (Jn. 14:6; Ac. 4:12; 1 Ti. 2:5).

Messiah A Hebrew word that means "The Anointed One." It means the same thing as the Greek word *Christ*. See also Jesus.

Mercy God's mercy and compassion to help those in need or in distress. God's mercy cannot be separated from His love, grace, and faithfulness. God's ultimate mercy was shown through His willingness to send His Son Jesus Christ as a sacrifice for the world (Mi. 6:8; Lu. 6:36; Ro. 11:30; Ep. 2:4; 1 Ti. 1:2; 2 Ti. 1:2; Tit. 3:5; 1 Pe. 1:3; 2:10; 1 Jn. 1:3; Jude 1:21).

Obey To do what you are told to do. To carry out God's commands. According to Scripture, God demands that His revelation be taken as a rule for man's whole life in both heart and conduct (1 Sa. 15:22; Je. 7:22; 1 Co. 14:21; Tit. 3:1). The disobedience of Adam and Eve plunged mankind into guilt, condemnation, and death (Ro. 5:19; 1 Co. 15:22). Christ's unfailing obedience "unto death" (Ph. 2:8; He. 5:8; 10:5-10) won righteousness (acceptance with God) and life (fellowship with God) for all who believe on Him (Ro. 5:15-19). Faith in the Gospel — and in Jesus Christ — is obedience (Ac. 6:7; Ro. 6:17; He. 5:9; 1 Pe. 1:22) — for God commands it (Jn. 6:29; 1 Jn. 3:23). A life of obedience to God is the fruit of faith (Ge. 22:18; He. 11:8, 17; Ja. 2:22). Unbelief is disobedience (Ro. 10:16; 2 Th. 1:8; 1 Pe. 2:8; 3:1; 4:17).

Paradise A perfect place. Another name used for Abraham's bosom or Heaven (Lu. 16:19-31; 23:43; 2 Co. 12:3; Re. 2:7).

Pardon The forgiveness of sins granted freely by God as a gift (Ro. 3:23) through faith in Jesus Christ (Is. 1:18; 43:25; Ps. 65:3; 86:5; Eze. 36:25; Mt. 6:14, 15; 18:21-35; Col. 3:13; 1 Jn. 1:8, 9).

Prayer Prayer is talking with and being with God. Through adoration, confession, thanksgiving, and supplication, believers are able to worshipfully communicate with God in order to build intimacy with Him (Je. 29:12; Ps. 102:17; Mt. 6:6; 26:41; Lu. 6:27, 28; Ph. 4:6; 1 Th. 5:16-18; Ja. 5:16; 1 Jn. 1:9).

Propitiation The removal of God's judgment on mankind through the death and resurrection of Jesus Christ (Jn. 3:16; 1 Jn. 5:3, 11).

Reconciliation Man is restored to God through Christ to friendship and harmony. When Christ died on the cross, He satisfied God's judgment and made it possible for God's enemies to reconcile with Him (Ro. 5:10; 2 Co. 5:18-20; Col. 1:20, 21).

Redemption The restoring of our fellowship with God through Jesus Christ's death and resurrection (Jn. 3:16-18; Col. 1:13, 14; He. 9:12).

Regeneration Believers are new creations through their belief in the Gospel of Jesus Christ as they commit and dedicate their lives to Jesus Christ (Jn. 15:4-9; 2 Co. 5:17).

Religion A fundamental set of beliefs and practices generally agreed upon by a like-minded group of people. This set of beliefs concerns the cause, nature, and purpose of the universe, and involves devotional and ritual observances. It also often contains a moral code governing the conduct of human affairs, also known as a worldview (1 Co. 2:1-5; Col. 2:8).

Repentance Confession of and turning away from our sin through the conviction of the Holy Spirit and turning to God for mercy through Jesus Christ with a desire to obey and serve Him (Eze. 18:30; Mt. 3:2; 4:17; Lu. 3:7, 8; 13:3-5; Jn. 16:8; Ac. 2:38; 3:19; 8:22; 17:30; 2 Co. 7:9, 10; 2 Pe. 3:9).

Salvation Salvation refers to the process of sinners becoming justified, sanctified, and glorified through the death and resurrection of Jesus Christ — deliverance from the physical and spiritual bondage of sin by God's grace through faith in Jesus Christ and His completed work on the cross. Salvation is a gift from God, by grace, through faith, and cannot be achieved through self-effort — but only through Christ (Jn. 1:12, 13; 3:1-18; 14:6; 17:1-5; Ac. 2:37, 38; Ro. 6:23; 10:8-10; 2 Co. 7:10; Ep. 2:1-9; Col. 1:13, 14; 1 Th. 5:9; Tit. 2:11; He. 5:9; 1 Pe. 1:18, 19).

Sanctification The completing to perfection the work begun in regeneration, and it extends to the whole person (Ro. 6:9, 13, 22; 1 Co. 1:30; 6:19, 20; 2 Co. 4:6; Col. 3:10; 1 Th. 4:3; 2 Th. 2:13; 1 Pe. 1:2; 1 Jn. 4:7).

Sin To disobey or displease God. Lawlessness (1 Jn. 3:4), the result of disobedience (Ro. 5:19), and rebellion (Is. 1:2) against God. Sin is unbelief (1 Jn. 1:10). The result of sin is death (Ro. 5:12). Jesus Christ is God's remedy for sin (2 Co. 5:21). Christ has saved us from the power, control, and consequences of sin, and from eternal separation from God (Ge. 3:1-19; Ps. 51; Ro. 3:23; 6:23; 1 Jn. 1:8, 9).

Soul A person's true inner self.

Theory A supposition or system of ideas intended to explain something, especially one based on general principles independent of the thing to be explained. A model (usually mathematical) that links and unifies a broader range of phenomena, and that links and synthesizes the laws that describe those phenomena. In science they do not grant an idea the status of theory until its consequences have been very well tested.

The Trinity The word *Trinity* is not used in the Holy Bible, but the concept is throughout. For example: **1).** Who raised Jesus from the dead? Well, it was God the Father (Ga. 1:1; 1 Th. 1:10); it was also Jesus Himself (Jn. 2:19; 10:17, 18; and it was the Holy Spirit (Ro. 8:11). **2).** Who gave the New Covenant? The Father (Je. 31:33, 34), Jesus (He. 8:1-13; 10:29; 12:24; 13:20), and the Holy Spirit (He. 10:15-17) gave the New Covenant. **3).** Who sanctifies believers? The Father (1 Th. 5:23), Jesus (He. 13:12), and the Holy Spirit (1 Pe. 1:2) sanctify believers. **4).** Who is the Creator? The Father (Ge. 1:1; Is. 44:24; Ac. 17:24; Ep. 3:9), Jesus (Jn. 1:3; Col. 1:16; He. 1:2), and the Holy Spirit (Job 33:4) are the Creator. **5).** Who indwells believers? The Father (1 Co. 3:16a; 2 Co. 6:16; 1 Jn. 3:24), Jesus (Jn. 6:56; Ro. 8:10; Ep. 3:17), and the Holy Spirit (Jn. 14:16, 17; Ro. 8:9, 11; 1 Co. 3:16b) indwell believers. *The Holy Bible* even describes this in terms of different combinations — Father and Son (Jn. 14:23), Father and Holy Spirit (Ep. 2:21, 22; 1 Jn. 3:24), and Son and Holy Spirit (Ga. 4:6).

Witnessing In the New Testament, believers are instructed to be good witnesses with both our speech and our lifestyle (Ga. 5:22, 23; 1 Ti. 4:12) — sharing our faith with others (Is. 52:7; Eze. 3:18, 19; Mt. 5:14-16; 28:18-20; Lu. 12:8, 9; Ac. 1:8; 1 Co. 3:5-9; 2 Co. 5:18-21; 1 Pe. 3:15).

Worldview A perspective of reality itself; a view of life; a comprehensive conception or apprehension of the world from a specific point of view. A worldview is a formal philosophy. The Christian worldview is consistent and non-contradictory and explains all the facts of our life's experiences. Every individual has a worldview, a perspective that both interprets and influences one's life. A worldview consciously or subconsciously answers four questions: **1.)** Who am I? (What is the nature of human beings?), **2.)** Where am I? (What is the nature of the world?), **3.)** What is wrong? (What is the nature of evil?), and **4.)** What is the solution? (What is the nature of good and salvation?).

Personal Notes

Personal Notes

Personal Notes

Personal Notes

_____

_____

_____

_____

_____

_____

_____

_____

_____

_____

_____

_____

_____

_____

_____

_____

End Notes

1. Josh McDowell, *The New Evidence That Demands a Verdict*, pg 4. Copyright © 1999, Nelson Publishers, Inc.

2. *The Holman Bible Dictionary*, pg 1035. Copyright © 1991, Holman Bible Publishers. All rights reserved. International copyright secured.

3. *Webster Dictionary*, 1828 Edition, *e-Sword*.

4. *Webster Dictionary*, 1828 Edition, *e-Sword*.

5. Dictionary.com

6. *The Expanded Vine's Expository Dictionary of New Testament Words*, pg 420. Copyright © 1984, Bethany House Publishers. All rights reserved.

7. Copyright © *International Standard Bible Encyclopedia*, *e-Sword*.

8. Copyright © *Smith Bible Dictionary*, *e-Sword*.

Deepen your relationship with God through a better understanding of His Word using LCMM materials (books and music) that glorify God, edify the Body of Christ, and reach a lost and dying world.

BOOKS

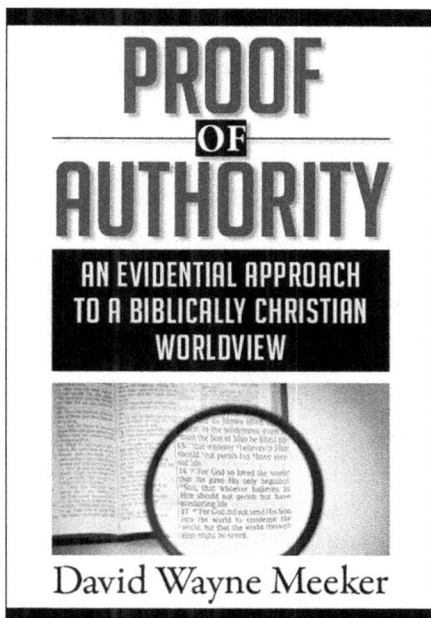

Proof of Authority: An Evidential Approach to a Biblically Christian Worldview Biblical Christianity is the only religion in the world that provides with its message *Proof of Authority*. God gives us overwhelming internal and external evidence in the coherency, accuracy, and unity of His word as it relates to our reality in validating His message. When you see all the evidence presented in this book, you will find a strong and irrefutable case for the Divine Origin and Inspiration of the Holy Bible.

Get your copy today at Amazon.com. Available in paperback $16.99, hardcover $21.99, and eBook $4.99.

The 70th-Week & Rapture Parallels

The 70th-Week & Rapture Parallels This book is a WORD to the watchful, and a WARNING to the wayward. Gain a comprehensive understanding of the events of the End of the Age. I parallel multiple Bible passages using Daniel's 70th Week as a chronological guide as we explore the unprecedented modern political and financial agendas promulgated by the United Nations and the BRICS International Financial Treaty. I explain how these events will, indeed, affect not only your present life but also your eternity! Get your copy today!

Available in paperback for $14.99 and eBook for $4.99 at Amazon.com.

Desires

Characteristics of True Conversion

David Wayne Meeker

Desires: Characteristics of True Conversion This book is a small book which invites the reader to explore and identify the cause, method, and effects of true conversion at a personal level. This is not a book about doing good works. Rather, this book is about the reality of the supernatural desires deep within our conscience which precede our good works. The Holy Bible clearly identifies the effects of true conversion as a spiritual turning away from sin and rebellion through repentance while simultaneously turning toward Jesus Christ for salvation. We will explore the cause, method, and effects of true conversion so that you can personally validate your conversion as being authentic. Get your copy today!

Available in paperback for $14.99 and eBook for $4.99 at Amazon.com.

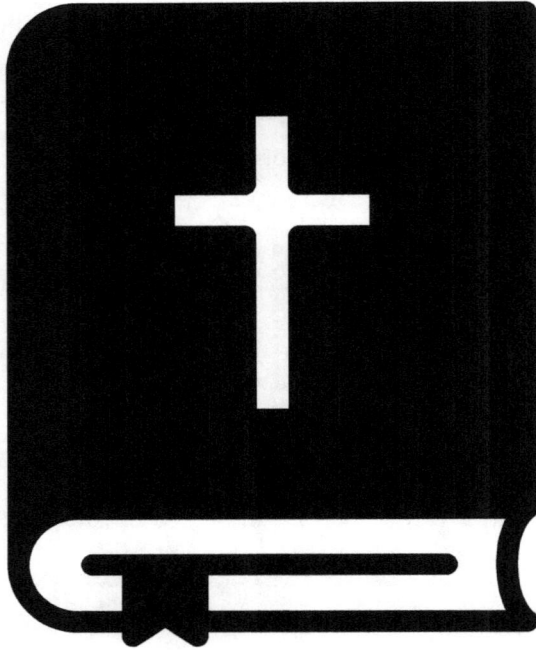

The Holy Bible is the most important Book you can ever read. Please contact Last Chance Music Ministry at lastchancemusic1@aol.com, and we will send you a copy of **The Holy Bible** at no cost to you. The price has been paid in full!

CHRISTIAN MUSIC

Played on Christian radio (KNLE 88.1 FM) in Austin, Texas.

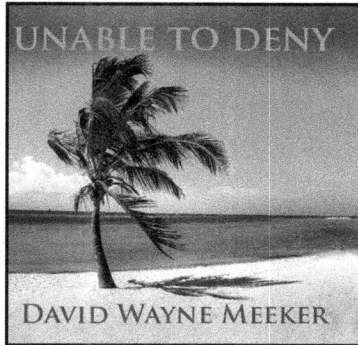

Unable to Deny CD: music available for digital downloads only.

Category: Christian Music. 10 songs total — all originals.
Available at digital music download sites, including Apple Music, Amazon.
com, Pandora, Shazam, Spotify, YouTube, Boomplay Music, Google Play,
and many more!

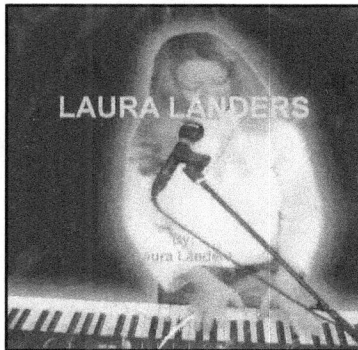

Laura Landers CD: music available at Amazon.com, Apple Music, Deezer,
Spotify, and YouTube.

Category: Christian Music. 12 songs total — all originals. Laura had this
album recorded before we got married, and it is one of my favorites!

www.ingramcontent.com/pod-product-compliance
Lightning Source LLC
Chambersburg PA
CBHW071826090426
42737CB00012B/2189